SOUL'S PERFECTION

⑨ ALSO BY SYLVIA BROWNE ⑥

BOOKS

Adventures of a Psychic (with Antoinette May)

Astrology Through a Psychic's Eyes

Conversations with the Other Side (available October 2001)

God, Creation, and Tools for Life—
(Book 1 in the *Journey of the Soul* series)

*Life on the Other Side**

Meditations (available January 2001)

The Nature of Good and Evil (available March 2001—
Book 3 in the *Journey of the Soul* series)

The Other Side and Back (with Lindsay Harrison)*

and . . .

My Life with Sylvia Browne (by Sylvia's son, Chris Dufresne)

AUDIOS

Angels and Spirit Guides

Healing the Body, Mind, and Soul

Making Contact with the Other Side

The Other Side of Life

Sylvia Browne's Tools for Life

(All of the above titles are available at your local bookstore.
Those without asterisks may be ordered by calling
Hay House at 760-431-7695 or 800-654-5126.)

⑨ ⑨ ⑨ ⑥ ⑥ ⑥

Please visit the Hay House Website at: **hayhouse.com**
and Sylvia's Website at: **sylvia.org**

SOUL'S PERFECTION

Sylvia Browne

HAY
HOUSE

Hay House, Inc.
Carlsbad, California • Sydney, Australia

Published and distributed in the United States by:
Hay House, Inc., P.O. Box 5100, Carlsbad, CA 92018-5100
(800) 654-5126 • (800) 650-5115 (fax)

Editorial: Larry Beck, Jill Kramer • *Design:* Jenny Richards

Library of Congress Cataloging-in-Publication Data

Browne, Sylvia.
   Soul's perfection / Sylvia Browne.
      p. cm. -- (Journey of the soul series)
   ISBN 1-56170-723-6 (pbk.)
      1. Life--Miscellanea. 2. Spiritual life--Miscellanea. 3. Society of Novus Spiritus (Campbell, Calif.) 4. Spirit writings. I. Title.

BF1311.L4 B76 2000
133.9'3--dc21

00-044893

ISBN 1-56170-723-6

03 02 01 00   4 3 2 1
1st printing, September 2000

Printed in the United States of America

For my beloved Creators

Sylvia's Prayer

Dear God,

*Let this new spirit of enlightenment rinse out all guilt
and fear. We come to you, God, knowing that You know not
only our names, but our hearts, minds, and souls.
We want to learn our lessons so that we can make the
journey of life easier. We want to perfect faster than
we have throughout all our lives.*

*From this moment on, we will love ourselves and
others and let Your supreme love light the lamp of our souls.
We will be imbued with love, judgment, and the will to
get us on track and keep us on our perfection scheme.*

*We will truly be a light in a lonely desert
that enlightens many.*

❦ CONTENTS ❦

Acknowledgments

This project is the result of many people working very hard to make my dream come true. This text was carefully revealed for you during many thousands of hours of research. I give my thanks to two people, Larry Beck and Mary Simonds, for their hard work and dedication to my mission in life.

Introduction

THE SOCIETY OF NOVUS SPIRITUS is my church, located in Campbell, California. The tenets in this book are based on the philosophy of this church, which I founded several years ago. The knowledge contained in this book represents the integration of several sources of information. First, it reflects knowledge infused by my own psychic ability throughout many years. It also reflects my spirit guide Francine's tremendous knowledge of life's plan and of the Other Side. Additional knowledge was passed down from my psychic grandmother, Ada, which represents almost 300 years of psychic oral tradition. In addition, thousands of hypnotic regressions were done independently of the other material, yet it all came together like clockwork, validating it, filling in any gaps, and showing that there is a logical plan to everything God creates.

I think we as human beings have lived long enough with the so-called mysteries. As Francine says, if you can think of the question, your guides will give you the answer. Indeed, my faith, Gnostic Christianity, teaches that we must always continue to seek for our answers, because seeking is an essential process for spiritual growth.

I decided to make this philosophy public because of the reaction I receive so often: "I have always known this. This is what I have always believed, although I couldn't put it into words. I just felt that this was a truth that resonated in my soul as *right*." The philosophy, although extensive, comes without fear or condemnation. It comes with knowledge, but without dogma. I have always believed that everyone, no matter what their beliefs, should take with them what they need or want, and leave the rest. Only occultism is hidden, secretive, and controlling; you will find none of that in these writings. Of course, certain codes for behavior are innate laws of good by which we must all live— but the part of you that is God is individual in every way.

The work in *Journey of the Soul* has three voices. Of course my own is present, but I also have two communicating spirit guides, Francine and Raheim, who are the major contributors. Francine's voice is audible to me, but relaying her information orally is not the most efficient form of communication. By special arrangement with God, I am able to allow Francine and Raheim to take control of my body so that they can communicate directly with others. This is called "deep trance mediumship," which is best known through the works of Edgar Cayce. An interesting aspect of this ability is that I retain no personal knowledge of the words or actions that occur while I am in trance. For many years we have done "research trances," giving us the knowledge that fills these pages. Of course, we all learn by asking questions, so you will see many such inquiries appearing in italics throughout this work. This series is truly a journey of the soul, and I am so glad to have you along for the ride.

This material represents hundreds of hours of work, so when you read it, by no means feel that you are merely reading the faint musings of a simple medium in trance. Much of the knowledge that has been garnered is extremely deep, abstract, and esoteric; you will probably prefer to read much of it in short passages instead of all at once. I hope you enjoy it, and more important, I wish that if nothing else, you come away as I have, with a magnificent obsession to learn more, explore more, and delve deeper into the great theology that is just waiting for us to discover.

We in the Society of Novus Spiritus find that there is great comfort in walking together in our belief, loving God without fear or guilt. To learn is spiritual, because knowledge destroys ignorance, prejudice, and greed.

God bless you. I do.

— *Sylvia*

EDITOR'S NOTE: *To reiterate the information stated in the Introduction, the following text has three voices. Of course, Sylvia speaks, but she also has two communicating spirit guides, Francine and Raheim, who are the major contributors. Whenever the voice changes in the text, it will be marked. Also, throughout the portions authored by Francine and Raheim, there are questions that appear in italics.*

𝒮 Chapter One 𝒸

REASON FOR LIFE

Francine: I want to talk to you about the purpose of life. Now, from our earlier discussions,[1] we know the basics: We decide to incarnate, we pick our life's chart, and we decide to perfect our soul, but not for ourselves—two-thirds of our existence is given over for the experiencing of God. So all of you "warriors for God" will take on more difficult experiences in order to perfect.

When we discuss creation, we have to say "in the beginning," although there was no "beginning." But for your finite mind, let's use the word *beginning* to mean the starting point of physical life. It became apparent to almost every soul that the only way they were going to fully understand God's knowledge was to come into life—to come into the battleground of good versus evil!

The difference between *knowledge* and *experience* is inexpressible. It's one thing to be told about something (call this intellectual knowledge) and another to experience it (call this physical knowledge), especially through the many stages of your many lifetimes. In life, you experience the positive and negative aspects and nuances, including defamation, rejection, aloneness, racism, and prejudice of every kind. Then, finally, you come to what can be described as an elevated spiritual and neutral place.

Now you're going to find people in all walks of life who want to find "spiritual knowledge." This phrase sounds very simplistic, doesn't it?

Like Sylvia says so many times: "Do good work, help each other, and then shut up and *go Home!*" This sounds simple, but it will take many, many lifetimes to get it right.

Dark and Light Entities

All white entities come down in a white column of light. All dark entities come down in darkness.

This makes it very easy for us. Of course, even with our intelligence, we're not always aware of who's dark and who's light, unless we see them coming into being. It would be nice if you had eyes that were open in which you could look around a place and see those with a dark column or a white column. It would be much easier for you to differentiate between them, but most of you cannot do this.

The main purpose of life is to help other people combat the darkness that confronts them. Of course, I assume that you understand I'm referring to darkness in people's *souls*; this has absolutely nothing to do with skin color. I'm referring to inherent evil.

To combat darkness does *not* mean to do battle with it, cohabitate with it, or pull it into your circle. It *does* mean to look at it, push it away from yourself, and try to get those you love pulled away from its sticky, gooey "connivances." The world, as you must know, abounds with darkness. We have a huge challenge.

Surviving Life

To perfect one's soul is simply to survive life. That is the ultimate: to be able to keep standing and make it through to the end, regardless of how hard you're hit. No matter that your worst fears were realized, no matter what happened to you. To perfect is to survive—to not give up, not cave in, not despair.

Despair is a killer; it can lead to suicide. You must not drink your way out of life's pain or numb yourself. You need to be a reality-based person. I'm not talking about people who are on medication in order to stabilize a chemical imbalance; that's totally proper behavior.

I'm talking about people who go to addictive behaviors. That's tragic. Probably one of the worst spirits you can take into your body is alcohol, because, when abused, it numbs and dulls and keeps you from experiencing your life. To harm the physiological body, although it may feel satisfying, is wrong. Two things can happen as a result: Either your life will be elongated, or you're going to need another life. There are many ways to commit suicide in this life: Alcohol and other addictions are just as deadly.

Is an addiction ever charted?

Some people are told that they're predisposed to an addiction of one sort or another. Before they come in, a lot of people are very, very adamant in saying, "I can beat it."

They chart with the option for a very strong possibility, the same as a suicide does. They're warned; they're told. A lot of suicides that we see are people who have incarnated too fast. They didn't get any rest; they went back in too fast. They didn't listen to anything, and they're shell-shocked.

God only knows that enough of you are shell-shocked because you've had so many lives. For many, this is your last life, and you're really tired and worn out. That doesn't mean that you're going to take a gun and put it in your mouth. Such behavior always forces you to have more lives.

Survive life. Serve God.

Now I know that a lot of you, regardless of your religious background, have heard so many times that everyone is supposed to "serve God." Even in my life, we were told to serve the gods. As a small child, I used to wonder, *How do I serve God?* The answer I have found is this: You serve God by serving His people. You reach God in many forms and many facets by serving people. If you just serve yourself, you are gaining nothing spiritually. This has nothing to do with loving yourself. You'll find the love of yourself if you love other people. However, if you just serve yourself and express your love for God, that's not enough. It's so much better if you do more than speak it; instead, go about your daily work giving, caring, and spreading your truth and your spirituality, whatever that may be to you. At least in this way, your God-center touches other people. If you don't serve God by serving other people on this earth, that is not so much an atrocity, but *you* have missed an opportunity to serve God.

It is very easy, because of the way the world is, to say, "I can't be bothered. I want to crawl back in a hole. Let them all be whatever they're going to be. It's not my problem." If nothing else, your position is not to "save" the dark entities, because you can't save them. But certainly save the white entities who are beginning to despair. It's not that they're weak, but the darkness has a way of making despair come into the minds of white entities. It seems like such an endless task, but it's not. What you're trying to do is keep your "army" together so they don't freeze or falter or burn up or whatever.

People ask, "But don't you want to save the dark entities as well?" You cannot save the dark; God will. Maybe you can save the gray. You want to be a light in the world.

The "gray" entities are experiencing nothing but meanness and negativity. All they're doing is feeding negative energy back into the world. What good is that? I'm sure that God's concept of experiencing through us includes that, but certainly no goodness is being created.

So the meaning of life is *service*. The perfection of your soul is service—and so many times *without any applause*. If you come into life and expect applause, you're going to be terribly upset. Your only "kudos," as Sylvia calls them, are what you give to God, and what God knows you give—and those truths are between you and God alone.

Don't expect the world to eulogize you in lights, as you have seen with Sylvia. If that's what you're looking for, then you should know that they can make you a saint one day and a harlot the next.

That's all you can ever expect in this life. So maybe you deal with ex-husbands, people who are prejudiced against you, and people who hurt you. You only answer to God, Who knows where your heart is.

When you keep repeating that to yourself, then your strength increases a millionfold.

Your name may not be in lights here, but your name is certainly in God's Lights!

Is Earth's population increasing?

Yes. I see it so much, and you must see it in your world. Sylvia was saying the other night to me that she has never seen so many babies at the mall. You must see them, too—there are babies and babies and babies. War has nothing to do with it. The depletion of humankind is not as great as the boom that is coming in. The boom is coming in now because you're getting to the end of this period. The souls that did not finish up their "coursework," so to speak, have to come in now.

Seeing the Light

You're here to perfect your specific life theme (see Chapter 3). In each life, you can pick a different theme or you can keep the same one, especially if you think you haven't experienced it well enough. In your last life, most of you will touch on all the themes—Tolerance, Experiencer, and all the rest.

You ask, "Where do I fit? God, I've gone through so many." That really is it. If you look very carefully, you'll see that you always have one main life issue that confronts you. You have a lot of them if this is your last life. You constantly have difficulties put upon you, but be aware, and do a self-audit. In other words, say, "Wait a minute. Am I learning Patience? Is this Tolerance? Is this Experiencer? Have I now become a Pawn? Have I now become a Catalyst in this position?"

Those are the things, the *meaning* of perfecting your soul, that you have to go through. It seems so meticulously analytical, which it is, because you so carefully planned all of it.

I think that each day spent without some kind of audit of yourself is a day lost. "Was there one good thing that I did? Did I help someone with something spiritual?" It can be as small as reaching over and grabbing someone's hand. But when you get up in the morning, make up your mind that on that day, you're going to send energy to someone. You might even send a prayer out to a homeless person. You may give someone a sandwich. You may just call a person on the phone. You might talk to a client you're dealing with and give them a warm word.

A day without doing something for someone else is a day lost!

Now, let's say that you're very ill and are confined to your bed. That is a time in which you can be introspective. You can meditate. You can ask God to let you rest and get ready for the next weeks or months or years or whatever you have left. However, always keep this thought pivotal in your mind: The Holy Spirit is with you. You are doing something for the Higher Spirit.

Constantly ask, "Are my actions for a higher good?" All of your experiences should be for the Higher Spirit. All the calumny and profaneness that you have had to endure, all the battering you have had to go through—I promise you that all of it adds to your soul's perfection.

The phrase, "They have seen the light," has been bantered about from the early Christians on to the fundamentalists. It truly referred to seeing the white light of the Holy Spirit. The perfection of your soul is not only *seeing* the light, but *bringing* the light to others.

If you're just paying attention to your own light, you're not going to advance quickly. That doesn't mean that you have to go tromping up and down the street gathering up all types of people to come to church. If you can relieve someone from one day's guilt or one hour of pain, you've done something as far as ministering. You don't necessarily have to be a minister within any church. Just say to yourself, "I want to be a minister for God. I want to administer God's Light to people." To *minister* to someone means to "serve their needs." Show your truth to others.

It doesn't do any good if you keep your truth inside and don't show it to anyone. That doesn't mean that you have to shove it down their throats, but at least you'll know that you've given them your truth. You may be amazed that people are coming into the light on their own. It has nothing to do with being psychic. It has everything to do with being spiritual. *Spiritual* and *psychic* are synonymous. The more spiritual you become, the more psychic you become. That is absolutely a fact. That is the meaning and perfection of life—to reach the pinnacle of being spiritual and psychic, and having those meld together—not letting the world stop you, not making what the world does to you so important. That's one of the hardest lessons that you learn.

Your next thoughts are, *What about my job? What about my love life? What about my health?* I know all that is important, but it is so fleeting. It's like a flu that you have for two weeks, and the next day you don't have it.

Love Yourself

We're going to talk about behavioral modification. I think that all through your lifetimes, literally, you've been inundated with erroneous information. Then you come back Home (to the Other Side), and you return to your true beliefs. Then you go back into a life, and you're brainwashed into another set of beliefs. It becomes terribly hard to try to figure out what's right. You're inundated by all types of moralistic behavior, commandments, church rules, and law. Behavioral modification is probably the most simplistic.

Our Lord said, "Love your neighbor as yourself." Now, let me get more specific about that. Let me try to release some of the burdens of guilt you may have. There are people whom you cannot possibly like. Yet many times, because "Love your neighbor" has been given to you, you are convinced that it's wrong to dislike others.

It is wrong *not* to dislike. Let me tell you why. If you're going to like and care for every single person (I'm not speaking of love), there's something wrong with your personality. You're deficient in being a whole person. Whole people have decided likes and dislikes, paths in which they follow, paths in which they won't follow.

You must try to love everyone's soul and wish them the best. But you certainly don't have to like their behavior or actions. To stay around a person that you intensely dislike is wrong. It disintegrates that person and yourself. Many marriages, friendships, and family relationships are built upon trying to stay around a person that one cannot tolerate. This causes you guilt and heartache and stunts your spiritual growth. You're laboring so hard to be "perfect" for no reason. Again, Jesus recommends that you "pick up your pallet and walk away."

When you give someone advice (all human beings are filled with advice for everyone), don't ever give advice that you think will apply to *you*, or what *you* would like. Try to be objective. That is the most spiritual road. Whenever someone asks you for an opinion or advice, don't internalize it; rather, try to put yourself in that person's place. There, again, is a very *spiritual modification*.

Care more for yourself. Reward yourself. For one week, try to do everything that you wish to do just for you. For one week, try it. I guarantee that by the end of the week, you will not only be doing things for you, but you'll be doing more for other people than ever before.

Once you can love yourself, so much love begins to emanate. If you find that you're a person who doesn't like people, you're in great difficulty. Not only is your world filled with people, but where you come from is filled with people. The greatest challenge that you'll ever have in this life is to get along with other people. That doesn't mean having to like them or constantly give out more than is humanly possible. It means being able to discern how compatible with you others will be.

It's perfectly within everyone's normal behavior to release frustration, to show anger, and to show fear. Instead, far too many people suppress their emotions within their own body; a vehicle that does not work exactly as it should. You have a superconscious memory of a body free of heaviness, free of ills. That, in itself, causes frustration.

Do you know that Jesus did not like everyone? He did not like the Pharisees. He could not stand the courts. He could not abide the rulers of Rome. Yet he cared for all people. Do you understand that?

It's impossible for you to walk around constantly, truly loving everyone.When you try to love everyone, you've diminished the word *love*. You use the word *love* so much that when it comes to truly loving and caring, you have no way to express it anymore. Most of you,

I can truly say, "like" and "care" for others, but very few of you in physical life know what true love is. This is *not* because you're deficient. It's because on your plane of existence, it's nearly *impossible*. Infatuation is probably the closest thing, giving you a few brief months of what you feel continuously on my side, but it's still accelerated a thousand times more where I am.

Because you get a brief glimpse of this feeling with a partner, you're constantly looking for the next, in your slang, "fix." The older you get and the more worn down you are from life, the less it comes. Something else must replace it—some deeper knowing that you're finishing out your contract with God, then you will go Home.

If you're constantly bogged down with grief or what should have been or what was not, you'll stunt your spiritual growth. If you're constantly wondering what people think of you, you stunt your growth. Does this make you an uncaring, unfeeling human being? Maybe according to the world's norm, but not in the bigger scheme of life.

Every single one of you is individually alone, making your way on a well-defined path to get back where you came from. You may select partners and companions along the way, but as I've stated before, because of your physical body and because you cannot merge, every single one of you is isolated. We, your spirit guides, are probably closer to you than any human being can ever be.

Don't be so obsessive about the next day, the next year, money problems, and so on. You may reply, "But I have to live." Yes, you have to live, but things are only going to be one way or the other. Believe me when I tell you: Almost everyone survives the money worries, the business worries, the love worries. So much excessive time is spent worrying about what is already predestined by you and the other individuals anyway.

Money is a great deal like love. It's meant to be taken in and given out. If money is taken in and held, it does not reproduce anything. People become too terribly concerned about materialistic holdings.

People have asked me, "Am I too materialistic?" Almost every time, I have reiterated, "No." Very rarely have I seen a person, regardless of their holdings or houses or cars, who I feel is truly caught in material greed. Now, as far as possessions, people can get caught up in materialism by caring too much in almost a self-conscious way what people *think* of them. *That* is being caught in matter.

It is so simple. You care for the majority of people. You hope they care for you. If they don't, there are others who will. That's what makes you more spiritual.

Simplify

Quiet down the mind. Know that God, within and without, takes care of all things. Leave the door of communication open for us to enter. We can't get through very well when you're constantly obsessing over something, such as money or a love affair. Because your mind is filled with that, we can't break though the noise long enough for us to make contact.

You can be simplistic and still be very intellectual. This means caring for the smallest as well as the largest. It's a whole process of retraining your mind. Walk into your home, close the door, and be grateful that you have four walls that reflect you, whether it's an apartment or a house. Be grateful that you have a job that brings in money so that you can eat and live, that you have friends around you, and a beautiful country that allows you to get to the ocean or the mountains in a matter of hours.

I don't want to sound like many of the so-called gurus who have wanted you to become so simplistic that you blank your mind. I have been called very "Westernized," which I find very strange, because my philosophy is very "Eastern."

I believe in activation and passivity: activation in doing something with yourself, passivity in letting life pull you. Don't move upstream. Let the stream carry you.

Pushing against the flow of life also stunts spiritual growth, because the path becomes harder. You put one rock after the other into the path that you've chosen. Most of those rocks are created by you. Oh, yes, there are also external blocks to deal with. There are periods of grief, joy, and aloneness. But how you get through these times depends on your frame of mind. A positive frame of mind definitely makes the journey easier.

Think of when you were first romantically, mindlessly in love with an individual. At that point in time, in that heightened excitement, if your car would not start and you lost your job, you wouldn't care. Do you see what I mean? If you *did* care, it would be minimized. But let the glow of the infatuation wear off, and your car doesn't start and you lose your job—now you're in the pits of despair.

The only love affairs that last are those you have with God, yourself, and the deeply abiding and comforting love that you have for people around you.

Infatuation in your world is wonderful, but it must take, let's say, a lower priority than the comforting companionship. That's why so many people commit and uncommit, because again, they're looking for that gigantic thrill. It doesn't come that often, nor does it last.

People who only search for the infatuation thrill really do age before their time, because their bodies cannot sustain it. It's too much. If you remember well, the heart races, you have no appetite, your face flushes, you can't sleep, and your blood pressure elevates, too. You could not sustain that state. You would die.

When we see one of you in a state of infatuation, we can see you sparkle and flare all over. Do you know that when the infatuation dims, your aura turns gray for a while? After the infatuation comes a gray period. If you work through that, then you usually turn a bright green or a bright blue. That means that there's rejuvenation and tranquility taking place. Most of you show varied shades of green and blue or sometimes shades of maroon, meaning agitation and irritation.

You are electrical. You are in control of this electricity. You should try to "cement" your aura so that it becomes greener or bluer or maybe shades of green and blue. It should be confined close to the body, not flaring way out.

Life

Everyone has some affiliation with another person's trials, whether in this life or from a past life. Lives are really not that individualistic.

You may think that you're going through something very, very specific to you, but remember that someone, at some time, has gone through that identical trauma. They may not have handled it any better, but they have experienced it, nevertheless.

The more difficult your life is, the more that you're perfecting your soul for God.

How can we discipline our lives more?

Discipline is mostly behavioral. How you deal with your life is based upon acceptance. That's the biggest thing when it comes to discipline. People think they must watch their diet and exercise in some way, but those things are not nearly as important as *going with the flow* of life.

Most of your problems arise because you push against life instead of going with it. This is so simplistic that most people negate it. Discipline allows you to flow with life's stream. In other words, if a bad relationship occurs, rather than fighting or worrying, say to yourself, "I'll ride it for as long as I can. Then I'll simply jump off this car and get on another one."

People harangue situations literally to death, because they have, as Sylvia calls it, a "one-time" terminal mentality about everything. "If I lose this job or love partner, I won't get another. There will never be anything else." Of course there will. Most of the time, human beings are trying so hard to keep themselves from being uncomfortable—from grieving or wanting—that they *create* the exact situation they fear.

Does it really matter if you move from one place to another? Is it really that important in life's journey if there is a loss of someone that you'll eventually be with again? It's very hard to explain to human beings that *nothing is terminal.* Even though we may talk exhaustively about the Other Side and how everything eventually evens out, the frustrations build up.

Just begin to allow yourself to flow. That's a big part of centering the self.

Remember how you felt when you were first in love, and the glow of that first love? In that state, if your car were to break down or there was a gas shortage, it would affect you, but not very much. If you're not in a state of loving or not in a state of being glad every day just to be here and be perfecting, then everything will bother you—heat, cold, gas shortages, next-door neighbors, dogs barking, and children that talk back.

There's a certain amount of worry that comes from being in a physical body, but much too much of it is self-inflicted. Once the *need* for anything is removed, there's an abundance. The flow of life is a cardinal rule in the universe: If you don't hinder the way, the way will carry you. That applies to every human being. It's the same thing with pain—once the pain is accepted, acknowledged, and experienced, then it can be handled.

The fear of pain or the fear that accompanies pain is so intense. That's why no one's tolerance of pain is any different. Medical people talk about high or low thresholds of pain tolerances. No, that's not true. It's the *resistance*. Accept the total and complete knowing that God doesn't ever let anybody suffer needlessly.

If you feel that you must have a certain thing, there's nothing wrong with a zealous ambition to accomplish it.

Is it true that difficult children don't flow with life?

Well, you must realize that they haven't come into full maturity yet as far as knowing this, but it's the parents' job to "flow" with the child until the maturity factor takes over.

Parents will say, when the child is older, "I'm more patient now; I can handle it." Somewhere along the line, if a person ever says that, they have learned to flow. Learning to flow is the definition of patience.

People are so burdened with finances. God doesn't require anyone to have to live impoverished lives. This "give up everything and walk around with dirty feet" is *not* what God ever meant. An empty stomach is not conducive to prayer. The only feelings of discontent that you should ever have is if you're not flowing well enough with life.

Do you realize that 99 percent of your fears never culminate? Yet if even one thing or one tiny part of something that you fear comes true, then you'll say, "I knew it." Not only that, but this will augment all the fears you've ever had. Then you think you're psychic enough to "know" that everything you fear will come true. Yet they don't, and all you have now is a fear that you created by yourself.

Let's say that someone flunks out of school and is sent away. Everybody, for a brief span of time, would say, "Isn't that terrible? That person flunked out." But ten years from now, how significant is that? Do you remember back in school, there was always, always a bad person? Where is that person now? Are they directly entwined in your life? Are they affecting you? Yet for that brief span in time, everyone said, "I'm so glad I'm not that bad person."

Everything is transient. Everything is moving.

Einstein didn't flow with the tide.

Oh, not the tide of the masses—but he did specifically flow with his *own* tide. Edison and all such people were able to flow with their own tide. If you read or knew anything about Einstein, he didn't let anybody bother him.

March to your own drum. Someone's grief can be someone else's joy. It's like the old adage that comes from your side: "One man's meat is another man's poison." It might be terribly depressing to all of you if everyone liked asparagus. There wouldn't be any. If you take nothing else with you from this information, take the one truism that *all things do pass.* It is the most simple thing in the world.

The simplest rules—those you were born with—have been complicated by humans. They have become dogmatic, and not just in religions. I'm talking about the structure of morality or behavior.

If you think you're not a rebel, that's all right. Every one of you *is* a rebel in your own right because you think and feel. You're unique and different from any other spark that God created. However, your relationships and experiences are not that much different. You can't give me one situation that you've lived through for which I cannot show you someone who has lived an identical pattern. Whether it was being orphaned, experiencing a death or the loss of loved ones, or disappointment or rejection, there has been someone who has lived it, and maybe that person has one up on you.

It's so ridiculous how much the word *karma* is misused. Everyone lives a life with a physical malady. Almost every life, depending on how traumatic it is, will come under "attack"—either by your own mental processes or because of disease or circumstances. This is where phobias arise. If in one life you had a heart attack and you felt that things were not finished, you might develop a phobia about heart attacks.

Everyone has had a life in which they were rejected by a loved one, and a life in which they were accepted. You can play off either one, depending on the sensitivity of the soul. Everyone's lives run the same way. You've all had lives where you were alone, surrounded, famous, and dejected.

People will say, "Well, I've only had four." It doesn't make any difference. Within one lifetime, you've seen people go from riches to rags, rags to riches, from beauty to degradation, and from rejection to acceptance. You've had periods in which there was no money, and periods where there is much affluence. You've had periods in which you were ill and then better. But every one of you has spent a life in which there was some type of major deformity.

All of you have had a life as the opposite sex. Some men resent this, because in their "macho" minds, they can't believe they were ever "shrinking" females. And many women cannot believe that they could have been very strong, dominant men. However, you could not ever understand the duality of life unless you knew both sides of Creation. People who question their gender identities have usually spent many lives as the opposite sex. For example, a gay man has most definitely had many female lives.

The more advanced you become, the more your feminine and masculine sides rise as you need them. So even being a female, you will show masculine-dominant qualities and very prominent female qualities, and not get into nit-picking exactly which one you are today, masculine or feminine.

One of the worst things—which destroys natural discipline—is to feel that you are martyred, and to be judgmental and critical of others. People, no matter what happens, are not pleased with criticism.

Most of these "judgmentalists" are cross and cranky, and they always have something unpleasant to say. Judgment merely adds darkness to the soul. It's actually an emanation with the intention of annihilating another's ego. There are a lot of things that are worse than physical death. If you're around unpleasant, cranky, mean, cross people for any length of time and you have to live in close quarters or work with them, you should find a way to get away from them.

Is planning our life based on readiness?

Yes, many years are spent in planning an incarnation. The exception to this is a suicide, who must immediately go back into an identical situation. But for all others, the planning is seemingly endless work. We don't get exhausted, but in your framework, it would be exhausting to really discern the right parents, the right body, the right geographic location, what kind of defects you are going to have, what kind of jobs you may be geared for, what kind of childhood and mid-life you'll have, and when you're going to die. Also, your astrological sign is very important. That's why I don't believe in negating astrology, because you *do* pick a sign that is conducive to certain things, certain elements within the scene.

It's all written in your chart. Sometimes some of those things have to be modified with the help of the Council. [This is the body of advanced entities on the Other Side that can counsel and help us. The Council advises people on making their life's chart a reality; they ensure that it will fulfill their chosen goals. They ask us if we choose to go higher or to test something.] When you're in a perfect environment, you think you can do it all in one life. That is the problem we have in trying to modify. The self is higher, then. When you're in an exhilarated state, you think you can handle it all.

Think of yourself at your optimum degree of health, and someone says, "Would you like to swim back and forth across that lake?" You say, "Oh, I feel so great." You jump right in. After you get in and swim one stroke after another, it becomes very tiring. You don't know whether you can make it back or not. That is much the way life is.

Most of the counseling and orientation is, "Be careful. You're taking on too much." There is constant scanning and running back to master guides and the Council to talk about it and get approval.

Which is more important, our soul's past or our genetic roots?

Your soul's past. Ancestors have almost nothing to do with you, providing only genetics. That is such a small part of your perfection. Otherwise, everyone would be almost cloned. If genes were all-important, then you would be replicas of each other. Often, you're told that you're just like your grandmother, Sarah, or you're just like Uncle Harry. So you adopt this idea, and you become defined by it. But very little is determined by any ancestral roots. It's much more functional to track past lives.

Life with Others

Even though you may be struggling with certain maladies, be assured that not all of them come from internal sources. Most of you are dealing with a lot of external problems that may actually transfer into physical ailments. That should give you some peace of mind— it's not coming from your own soul!

You can choose to either absorb or negate this external bombardment. You know that I don't believe in a passive life. It's somewhat like the old saying about "water off a duck's back." If you're well oiled enough, you really are better protected from things that happen with loved ones, friends, and associates; you can even put up with parents, children, husbands, or whoever hurts you most deeply. If your soul is solid within itself, negativity will not strike the mark like it used to. You will understand everything in God's own time.

In any love relationship, one carries the responsibility for the love, and one does the loving. If the relationship sours, neither one is at fault, but the aware one carries responsibility for the karmic evolution of both. It's that person's responsibility, if they're to perfect, to have a deep understanding and tolerance of what is going on. I don't mean that if someone hurts you, then you should thank them. I would expect you to kick back. You don't need your temple defiled.

There's a lovely prayer that Sylvia has always liked so much. It goes something like this: "My soul is the land on which my house is built. There shall be no trespassing, looting, pillaging, or plundering on this, my land." Once the dignity of your soul rises up high enough, you won't be victimized anymore. You can't be. No one can victimize someone who refuses to be a victim.

If you keep screaming, "Why does this happen to me?" then listen: It's because you've let it sink in too deeply. That doesn't mean that you should be a robot, but your faith can expand to a point where you realize that you might have been just a target that they used. It was not necessarily directed toward your ego. You might simply happen to be in the way of a roller coaster, bank robber, or abusive man. If you happened to get in the way, you might get it. Everyone standing by says, "There's an innocent bystander." You can be an innocent bystander in your own family or job situation and become a target.

If someone wants to put you on a cross, you don't have to hang there. If we in life could not be victimized, no one would stalk anyone. I don't mean the person who has murdered or killed. I'm talking about things worse than that. Ego and soul trauma are far worse than any murder, rape, pillage, or plunder. Rejection is probably one of the worst target situations.

It's all in the plan that it would get worse before it would get better. You chose to come down in one of the hardest times. *You will not fail.* Almost all of you are on your last life, anyway. One thing I can assure you of is that almost no souls ever go backward. All go forward—maybe an inch at a time, maybe in micrometers, but we all go forward in life. Otherwise it wouldn't be worth it. Don't you remember in school that you might have sat in a class that you didn't understand at all, and you daydreamed through it? But you absorbed *something.* You might not have thought you did, but you were there, putting in your time, and something seeped in.

Nothing is lost. Nothing is ever lost.

Human beings carry within themselves heaven or hell—sometimes both. I think that children should be taught at a very early age that they have the power to create either a very happy life or a very disastrous one. That's the reason some people can go through a traumatic situation and come out whole, while others crumble at the slightest thing. They've never found within themselves the control factor or the supremacy of their own God-center to know that they'll survive no matter what is sent to them. Nor do they know that they have the power to handle everything by themselves.

We watch people continually propel themselves into the most horrendous situations. If you look back, you can usually tell when you started down this desperate track. If you're in control of yourself, you have the ability to ride the difficulties more easily.

The greatest truth is to be true to yourself. There is nothing more important than this.

An example of that would be living a lie—not being true to what you believe is true—by living with someone or a situation that you can't tolerate, in which you have to be hypocritical; or living in a family or job situation or anything else that you didn't believe in. I'm talking about adulterating your own soul—being untrue or unfaithful to your own soul.

I've noticed, though, that Jesus is walking the world more than ever before in a *real* state. However, I want to clarify that he is *not* showing up on Ouija boards. Jesus' presence is stronger in the world than it has ever been before.

God's power now descends more rapidly than it ever has before.

The world can be quite a humorous place if you can observe it from behind the eyes of your soul, which cannot be harmed. Things can roll off more easily if you adopt the attitude that "this too shall pass."

How important is it to suffer for the moment? How important is grief that extends beyond the point that it should? How important is a little pain—is it important enough to scar your soul? The soul's essence *can* be scarred.

That doesn't mean that you can't be healed when you come Home to the Other Side. You can be cocooned and sleep for a while. But that's like going on a marvelous journey, going back to see all your old friends, and being too tired to even enjoy it. If you had waited many years to go back to your homeland and you felt sick when you got back, that would be very disappointing, especially when everybody is there and wants to have a party. Then, of course, you don't have what you might term "jet lag," because when you come over to the Other Side, you feel weightless, almost as if you're in water. You know how marvelous that feels? There is no pain.

Those who are more spiritually evolved do not have a transitional problem on the Other Side, because it's a remembered thing, like riding a bike or driving—you never forget it. Please try to assure your friends, if they are in pain or sorrow, that nothing lasts forever—certainly not life. If you don't believe that deep within your soul, you're going to fall into fear. It may even be hard for you to believe that something will not always be. Especially if pain or grief hits, it seems like it will always be there, even for the most advanced souls.

I'm sure that the grief of losing a loved one never totally goes away. It just shifts into another position. The need, loneliness, concern, and love just transforms into a love of other people. Of course, the loved one never really left. In fact, they're closer than they've ever been, but now they're out of sight.

One really never gets over grief. One learns to convert it into something else, perhaps helping cancer patients or working in schools. The world is cruel in expecting grief to end. You're not only grieving consciously, but on a subconscious level as well.

Part of the anger about death comes subconsciously—"You're gone, and I'm not." When some people are dying, they slowly retract from even their loved ones. This is another type of anger, leaving the people they love. Anger starts welling up. It's such a shame that we can't convey to people how lucky they are to be going Home and really mean it.

Convey that truth: "You are going Home. Your work is finished. You are graduating."

Life Is Work

Sylvia and I have talked about this issue extensively: *Quit* hoping that life is supposed to be marvelous. Life is work.

Unfortunately, all entities come in with the idea that life is sup-posed to be happy and loving—the great love and the new car will come along. I don't want to make you nonmaterialistic, because those things do bring a great amount of comfort, and you have a right to nice things. But if you don't get them, it truly is not the end.

It's like being in a school that you don't like, but you'll eventu-ally graduate and get through it. If you never have a partner in your life—or a child, the newest car, or the best house—your *soul* will not die from this. You may make it harder for yourself by wishing and feeling that you deserve to get it. Just know that your spiritual wis-dom is more important than any *thing*.

You have a right to graduate from life, and to be as happy as you possibly can to survive life. Just that in itself is perfection.

If you would really, in your soul, take each day realizing that all things pass, you can become more peaceful. Just accept the idea and the belief—it's not faith—that you are here on a mission of spiritua-lity, whether through a church or otherwise.

You are here to join hands along the way, to find a friend or a group of friends who care and who will be with you. If you do, you would not feel so unbalanced. You could better sustain the grief of loss without becoming an android, because after all, you are the emo-tional side of God. You will experience emotion, although it's some-times painful.

Life is like getting a shot. You know it will hurt somewhat, but it's for a greater purpose. It won't last forever, and the needle will be taken out. Sometimes when pain is felt, the mind believes that it will always be there. But, of course, it, too, passes.

When you're very sick and someone says, "You'll be better in a week," you may respond, "I hope so," even if you really don't believe it. Nor can you remember a time when you weren't sick, unless you can rise above the physical. I don't mean that you should negate or punish your body and just love the spiritual. No, you should cleanse, care for, and be good to the body, giving it comfort. After all, it's the temple of the Holy Spirit. But to base so much on what is externally happening with your car, boyfriend, wife, or children—how small and insignificant that brief and tiny vignette is to the whole scope of your perfection. Adopt that attitude, even if you don't believe it at first. The real feelings will come later.

Everything washes away except for your purpose and your mission.

Without following a bright star, you'll never find any real contentment. When you planned to come into this life, no one guaranteed you that you would have a happy time. You didn't guarantee it for *yourself*. That is most important. The part of God within *you* chose it.

Then you gripe about it—that's also part of the human condition. Don't judge yourself for small misdemeanors. Don't take it harshly into your soul if someone rebukes you. It can only make the soul stronger if someone embarrasses you or tears you down. Being in the spotlight, positively or negatively—how much can that hurt you?

We carry these "negative implants" far more than any of the joy that people give us, saying, "That was so awful. I'll never forget that." Very rarely do you ever hear, "That was so beautiful. I'll never forget that." I don't mean that you don't have a right to feel embarrassed or hurt. Life has a way of making you feel sometimes like a criminal or a dunce—like you're crazy.

There is a difference between feeling and being.

Do we retain this knowledge to avoid the same mistakes?

Oh, you forget nothing from this life or past ones. If you've forgotten it consciously, you haven't done so subconsciously in your own Akashic Records (the vast repository of all events for all time). If by chance you start to repeat a mistake, then your subconscious—the Guardianship of the Mind—can stop you. But only if you listen to your first impression..

A pattern repeats until we learn from it fully. Then, it's not that you're without feelings, but any trauma will be transient. Consider your Christmastime—it's marvelous when you put your tree up, but afterward, how much do you remember the tinsel, the lights, and the balls? These physical memories are fleeting, whereas the emotional memories make a lasting impression. When a thing is broken, you feel bad for a while, but how long can you suffer from it? You won't live out the rest of your days vowing never to forget the day it was broken.

When a desire is thwarted, some become bitter and angry over it. If children don't turn out the way you think they should but seem to be on a destruction path; if your spouse doesn't love you as much as you feel he should; or a loved one has rejected you—how important is all that after it's past? You felt it and learned from it; it happened, so move on.

Every soul is singular in its mission. Every soul has a purpose. Souls may link up for a greater purpose, but their journey is still singular.

Where does our responsibility end?

You *can't* be responsible for the karmic evolvement of another soul. When a person begins to hurt and affect *you,* then responsibility has ended, even if your goal is incomplete. Many times, as a parent or relative, you take on too much responsibility for someone else's evolvement.

You've been programmed into believing that you must continue, caring *far beyond* the point when you should still care—to a point where you can no longer function. The person who is seemingly on their own path of destruction may, in the bigger scheme of things, be evolving in the way they should. Yet you have ceased to evolve.

Social programming—feeling that you "should" worry and suffer for another—is only part of the incarnate state. Of course, you feel and care—but how long can you keep bludgeoning yourself?

The most aware people carry the most evolvement. But caring when your hands are tied is different. You came down with the express purpose of learning to feel and care, but you also need to keep it in its proper place. All else may fail, but your beliefs, your structure, and your soul will not.

Children should be blessed and then released. The relationship with children should be to live and let live. A human being, young or old, will not change their course of action until they're ready, and of course, when the student is ready, the teacher appears. Someone with greater energy will appear, such as a psychiatrist, psychologist, teacher, or another mother or friend. But until the person is ready, this type of catalyst will not do any good; nothing will. However, they are, of course, far better for having met the catalyst.

So you can be right in the path of someone who has a problem with alcohol, drugs, self-mutilation, or self-degradation. You can't help that person unless, within their soul, they really want to be helped. Of course, there are certain rare people who can reach in and trigger sparks that people don't even know they have.

We planned our life on the Other Side, but we bit off more than we can now chew?

That's because you were feeling absolutely marvelous. Think of the best that you've ever felt in this life. If someone said in that split second of euphoria, "All right, now, we're going to tattoo your arm," you'd say, "I can handle that," until you got into it. Then after three or four sticks of the needle, you'd say, "Wait a minute. I don't feel so good anymore."

An adage applies here: "Your eyes are bigger than your stomach." To look down from the positivity of my side—the totally beautiful, non-ego-structured environment—life problems always seem trivial. It's like a mother going through childbirth. Not that it's all that horrendous, but she forgets very quickly what it was like—until she's in labor again. Then she remembers.

Why don't we remember how hard it is?

Because otherwise, you would *never* choose a life. You see, it's like picking a college or high school. They may tell you it's hard, and you know you have to go, but you're really sure that you can handle it until you get in there. There is a divine part of you that needs to evolve, to thrust forward and come into this negative environment and become stronger through adversity.

The more stable your soul and the more lives you've lived, the more you'll feel that nothing is more important than finding your purpose in life. This doesn't mean that home and family or loved ones aren't important—but spirituality becomes more important.

You don't think, on the Other Side, that you can fail. How many times have you done something that others didn't believe you were capable of? And you said, "Oh yes, I can." Then, maybe you got into it and wished that you had never said that.

It's the same thing. On my side, you have all the energy and vitality to start out with, until you got into the day-by-day grind of it. Besides, over here, everything is weightless, timeless, and beautiful. It's hard to remember the pain of life in that kind of environment.

Are we warned not to do so much?

Most counseling guides tend to advise restraint. They will try to reduce your goals—especially when an entity gets too ambitious or if it backs down too fast. The guides tell them to be very careful and watch certain danger points most of the time, unless they're very experienced.

But people have a tendency to really believe that this time, "I'll do it. This time I'll climb the mountain. I didn't last time; my lungs hurt. Well, I wasn't in good shape. This time I can really do it," until you get halfway up again. Then you get the burning in your lungs, and your legs get weak. There you are again.

Do we have to accomplish great things?

Oh, you already *are*, because you're surviving. You don't have to climb big mountains. Just to survive is enough. At one time or another, we've all climbed that big mountain.

You don't need to struggle so hard, because your life is well charted. Whatever you really need will appear. It will come right up out of the ground in front of you, if necessary.

Some self-destructive people appear to be wasting their whole lives.

To you it may seem that way, but they might be here as a catalytic force to perfect everyone else around them.

What about suicide?

Well, suicide is, of course, a very negative exit point; it's never advocated in any way. It's never an intrinsic part of the plan. Usually it's what we call an emergency code going off. The soul must immediately do it all over again. No one ever escapes by suicide. That person just has to come right back in with all the trauma and depression. They go right back into another life that's almost identical.

You can never say that a suicide is a pawn situation, as murder is. Nothing is ever lost, because other people can learn from it. But a soul doesn't pick a suicide to help others learn. No. It's a fluke. It breaks your contract with God.

When they go to the Other Side, suicides are immediately cocooned. That means just exactly what it sounds like: We wrap and suspend them right away, and they sleep. We make them go back right away. This is the only time that there is any intervention, because it's the only flaw that appears. Usually, what you think is "right away" can be 40 or 50 years in your time, which to us is not long.

Do we consciously remember a suicide?

When a soul has committed suicide, very rarely do they ever attempt it again. They remember very well. Most entities do not commit suicide. It really is the minority rather than the majority.

As you go through different relationships, seek to understand that any type of grief or problem is always incurred from relationships with other people—even debt. Why did you get into debt? Because you were trying to please someone else. You were trying to reward or show off. Your entire lives deal with such interactions.

When enlightenment comes, it can have unexpected consequences. As you begin to see why you put yourself through so many things, you might need to dissolve some relationships. But don't come away, then, feeling like, "Why did I put up with this for so long?" With knowledge comes understanding.

The only thing I want to do is help you understand your soul's evolvement, without grief. If you've accomplished a little bit of that, you've made the road easier for yourself.

Why do some individuals stay in unpleasant situations?

You must really grit your teeth then, when there is no longer any joy and it has become a chore. You're not learning anything, but only setting up a negative rebellion in your own soul, and it's not creating any good for the other party either. Realize that, in the final outcome, all relationships are transient. When the two of you come back Home, you'll understand it.

Now, please be clear on the difference between the simple release of everyday griping and the seriousness of needing to leave someone. I'm referring to when it gets to be a real burden to the soul, and you're no longer functional because you're so upset.

People love to complain about their hardships, but watch their actions. Are they functioning, going about their work? Are they still basically enjoying life? Then it's just a release of tension. When it begins to be depressing and the person begins to stoop from the burden of it, it's no longer serving anyone.

That's where the false ego arises. "I'm the only one who can help this person. If it were not for me, no one else could do it." This statement is never true: There will always be someone else to do it. No one is ever indispensable.

Things that are done out of love, for their beauty, should remain your quiet secret with God. It really is the way churches used to say: "Rewards are gained *after* this life." You don't need them now, regardless of how tremendously self-sacrificing you are. By publicizing your good deeds, you're really cheapening the reward that you should get later. It's like having too many wedding ceremonies throughout your life. If you keep going through it, it loses the joy, the beauty, the thrill, the excitement.

Living Your Life

I want to talk to you about true spirituality and give you some methods by which you can combat the darkness and the lack of prosperity that seems so commonplace in your world now. I want to talk to you about *living* your life.

You spend most of this life—as you have past ones—trying to find a place of happiness and a person to be with. I won't dwell on how much you should love yourself, because that's been too overworked. But I want you to think of yourself as a solitary entity, totally imbued with every survival mechanism and resource at your disposal. You were sent, like a bullet, down a chute to enter life.

You come upon this planet of negativity, adversity, greed, calumny, and slander. In your journey, you begin to feel that you want and need another individual. You go from mother to sibling to teacher to, later on, a partner. All of those things are acceptable, but they're far too overrated. At last, you evolve to a point where you realize that everyone in your life can add something, but that you must walk your journey alone—then, you are truly advanced.

This doesn't mean that I don't believe in what you call the "sacrament of matrimony." Of course I do, because we have a similar concept on my side, in our twin souls, or soulmates. In either relationship, people who are able to live comfortably within themselves—and stop constantly looking for that "other self"—are happier and farther along the spiritual road than are those who constantly want to know where their other half is, or who need someone in their life.

Please realize that through your many lifetimes, you've probably been with hundreds of people. Stop and be realistic. How many people do you think you were really attached to? Many.

When we all get together on my side, there is a reunion. I cannot explain to you the magnanimousness of the loving of many. Your physical bodies are limited to loving one person at a time. All through your life you're searching for a perfect mate, although you yourself may not be perfect.

Be solitary inside yourself.

This doesn't mean that you're not supposed to give out love, because you can do both. But do not attach to another person so much that you feel that there's nothing beyond that person. Very rarely do soulmates ever incarnate into life together, for the simple reason that they're too empathetic with one another.

You may say to me, "Then maybe we should all live in convents." Oh, no. Live in the love of God and yourself, totally and completely. Love another human being unconditionally. As Sylvia says, "Be in the state of becoming more loving."

You never have *become* anything in this life. You are in the state of becoming advanced spiritually, God-centered, and free of phobia. When you get hurt enough, tired enough, and are too much into life, you start getting phobic. So you start living under self-imposed conditions: "I'm afraid of water, heights, people, aloneness, or animals."

The more we have conditions put upon us, the more conditions we put upon others, and the more phobic we become. The more we expect others to live up to some standard, the more fearful we become. As our world gets more narrow, there are no more windows. At this point, we begin to fear the dark, and fearful things begin to spring up in the shadows. That is the law of life.

You came into life with true beliefs, true knowledge—all the marvels from the Other Side. As you get into life, they begin to fall away from you. Haven't you had some days that were so long that you forgot how cozy it was in bed? Haven't you had years that were so long that you actually forgot what Christmas was like the previous year? This is just in this lifetime. Don't you see how the Other Side begins to get so vague?

Life wears and tears at you. It's the greatest and most sublime of tests.

If you want to advance quickly and not come back, then you absolutely *must* incarnate at some time. Everyone, in order to perfect, must come down to what we call the training ground, the boot camp, the school.

We come down into life with all the knowledge that we're supposed to remember. But the minute the pressure, air, and gravity hit us, we forget. On a real physics level, your atmosphere is denser, thicker, and heavier than ours. You might say that we're much more *rarefied* than you are.

You start out with one purpose to fulfill, your theme, against any odds that you've set up. The variations of experience are uncountable. When you see people planning for their lives, they sit with rooms full of people intricately charting out how they'll meet this person; how they'll give someone else a checkpoint; where to be born, etc., etc., etc.

People will be messengers for you. A friend may say, "In case I'm out of line, by the time I'm 39, walk up to me, and say something." It's a colossal play on a stage. It's wondrous. Millions of lives light up. If we were to put this on a gigantic screen with millions and millions of lights, they would synoptically point and trickle down to the other lights.

It's marvelous for us to watch it on the big boards. We have gigantic scanners. I know you might find that to be truly amazing—that we have technology where I am—but you would never even believe our technology. You would think it's out of some sci-fi movie. We can chart you on a board, on records, and on scanners. Many times, in the astral state, you come back and check your progress yourself.

When a person has taken their own life, they usually had been counseled, helped, and told not to come into life, yet they did anyway. Their light flickers and drops. It's the most amazing thing to see two other lights reconnect to keep the line straight.

Sounds like a road map, doesn't it? In a way, it is. It is millions of people in a gigantic enterprise playing out their parts, testing themselves against the worst challenges. Life is a game of test and skill. You play it as if it were the only game. Some win, some lose, but there's always another game somewhere in the universe.

Say to yourself during the day, "This is a game." The word *game* connotes cruelty or frivolity, but this is a serious game of gain, of solitary evolvement toward perfection. If you don't connect with this image, then simply know that it's all passing.

Think for a few moments. Let your mind expand, and think of all the people who have died before and during your life. Think of them filling this room—all of them crowding in, because there are no walls to us. How many do you think there would be standing? Millions. You would be standing, too, because you've lived many lives and died many deaths. You are so fleeting and temporary in life, but you take it so terribly seriously.

Sylvia says, "You will fulfill what you charted to fulfill, whether you like it or not." There is a "guardianship" inside you that you have never been told about. It is a failsafe that, unless it has been damaged, takes you clear through to the end of things no matter what. Science has called it instinct, survival, and genetics. It's more like a throttle. Sometimes it goes fast; sometimes it goes slow.

Will your mind stay the same on the Other Side? Of course it will, so drop all the fear. Everyone who has had a near-death experience always says that the one thing they had was no fear.

You may be saying to yourself, "I have no fear," yet you do. No one in a physical body has *no* fear. Life is fraught with phobias. But in death, the absence of fear happens instantaneously. Fear is only known in a physiological form. The more you tell yourself that, the more you're going to find that you're closer to your own God Consciousness and God-center.

The only thing to fear is fear itself. That saying is true. But it should go further: Fear unto itself *should* be feared because it can become an actual physical force. After you've lived your life, you come back to the Other Side, where you're absolutely aware that there's no fear. You go directly to the Hall of Wisdom, where you and your guide sit down and look at a scanning apparatus with which you can go through your life.

You've heard people say, "My whole life flashed in front of my eyes." Many people right before death really trip into these scanning mechanisms, although no one sits and watches. In the scanners, there's no overhead voice judging, "You really were bad here." No. You sit and view your life, with your guide or alone, as you choose. Many times people flag certain parts of their life to show their friends later. There is constant researching. You will see groups sitting around and viewing parts of their lives, talking to each other about what could have been done better to help the spirituality of the person.

Everything is done without ego. You don't see people required to justify their position. They're truly interested in how they could have done it better. Now, all this is personal, so not one other entity ever has to know, unless you wish it. No one puts your life on display and holds you up for ridicule. That would never be done anyway. In truth, no one holds you up for ridicule more than you do yourself.

There aren't many beliefs you must come upon, but for your own spirituality, you must know that you do *not* have a judging God. The only thing that God is made of is wisdom and love.

After you've scanned your life, you meet with your friends, although this order is sometimes reversed. We know when there's a person entering from any part of the globe, both because we're told telepathically, and because, you might say, we know that the train is coming in by the light that flashes. Everyone is in attendance to meet you.

People may say that someone "died alone." Not a possibility. Not only was their guide there, but the chance that this was their first life is about a million to one. Any number of former relatives and loved ones could be waiting to greet them, even your beloved animals.

I want to give you a beautiful visual. Picture a high mountain with stunning pines. Now I want you to think of yourself going above the tree line. As you ascend past the forest, the trees get more sparse, maybe a little bit thinner and farther apart. As you get up higher, the light becomes more iridescent and translucent. You feel yourself spiritually advance to a high, rarefied place where there are fewer trees, but they are more beautiful and shiny.

I remember explaining this to Sylvia one day back when things were harsh. I said, "That's all right. You're moving beyond the forest line; you're now getting to the point where maybe there's just one tree." Sylvia replied, "And a lightning bolt just struck that one."

Another beautiful meditation deals with the top of a pyramid. Here, you're pulling in ancient symbols. In this life, if you ever really want to see the Other Side, try to visualize a window in the shape of a pyramid. That symbolic object pierces through almost anything. Sylvia uses the pyramid to represent the superconscious and the mind structure; it's a symbol used by the ancient Aztec-Inca culture as well as the Egyptians.

Think of yourself ascending to the top of a golden pyramid to bring about the solitary emanation of your own soul. At the top, have a beam of golden light shoot right through your heart. You will find that it cleanses and brings forth the "self" faster, and certainly helps you to love unconditionally.

Also, I want you start writing in a journal about all the people, objects, and animals in your life that you could possibly want to love unconditionally. Don't be discouraged if you find it hard at first, because all of those people are steps along the path to spirituality.

Your pace through life is always adjusting itself. But it doesn't do any good if you're unaware. Of course you will still graduate if you're not aware, but do you really want to get a D instead of an A+? With a D, you're going to have to come down again or go into an option life, because you don't feel finished. [An option life is "extra credit for your soul. After you've fulfilled your personal contract with God, some folks will come back for additional incarnations for the betterment of humanity. Since the requisite time incarnate is finished, these lives are called "optional."]

I want to tell you, my dear friends, you don't want to come into life again. If you haven't figured that one out, you'd better come to grips with it. There is no one I know who does. Even though we on the Other Side do not experience sadness and pain, the closest we come to it is when we see *you* going into life. If you think there's grief in your world when someone passes, you should see how you are when going *into* a life!

People on the Other Side will stand by the chute for what you might term "days," run to the scanners, and be "highly concerned" about the pain their loved ones are going through. Because, you see, we are still of the same essence and personality. However, don't feel that we're unhappy over here. It's not the same kind of unhappiness that you would feel. Remember when I told you that the "big board" is lit up and we're all connected? Yes, we're all connected from the Other Side, as well as connected here, too.

We are all interconnected.

When one falls and is hurt, when one light goes out on the "big board," all the other lights flicker. You've been told that "you are your brother's keeper," and you truly are. When you fold or don't fulfill your contract, you diminish everyone around you.

You may ask, "Doesn't that give me guilt and responsibility?" Well, life is responsibility. In deciding to come in, you took on a tremendous responsibility. That's why people have a right to do almost anything, but they do *not* have a right to remove themselves from other human beings. That doesn't mean that you can't be solitary, but you must interact with other human beings.

Oh, in grief or sometimes when you're trying to identify yourself, you must retract somewhat. But you can't stay inside yourself. This is the surest way to illness and insanity.

Going out into a lonely desert and staying there for ten years is not perfection. That's cowardice and laziness. I have never seen a chart with that written in it. That is a fluke where somebody was supposed to go to a desert for a few days, and they elongated it. You have a lot of room in your chart for variation, but not deviation.

Please remember that when people talk about the "higher self," it only means the most noble and spiritual part of you—it is still you. You are in full essence down here. There is no part of you somewhere else floating around. You're not in some other lifetime. You are in full essence now—mind, body, and spirit—but don't become Earthbound. Be above your physical self. You are *in* the body, but not *of* the body. You actually reside not in the body, but about four inches above it. Your soul is manipulating the body simply to get around this world in order to fulfill your contract.

You're not in the engine of the car, are you? You're behind the steering wheel. If you were in the engine, you would burn up. That's what happens to so many of you: You get into your body, and you burn up. You can't see where you're going. You can't see the road. So get back behind the wheel where you're supposed to be.

Let me tell you what I've observed. I've never helped Sylvia in the reading room [where she does her psychic readings], but I've certainly seen a lot. More times than not, I've seen that when a person lets life pull them, rather than activating themselves, it's far better for the person. I don't mean that you *just* let life pull you, but when you're in a confusing situation between two issues, don't do anything. Let life react. People who are spiritual, especially, think they should make decisions instantly. Yet the only commitment or decision you have to make is to be more spiritual. Meditation is listening to God, and prayer is talking to Him. Knowledge makes you more spiritual.

Do you keep your same personality on the Other Side? Of course you do. Now, some of you won't like this, because there are certain personalities you just don't like. That's all right, because unlike your side where everybody is lumped together, here, each personality finds a compatible group. Not everybody becomes introverted or extroverted or a comedian or actress. Some people would never want that.

If there's a secret desire in your heart that you couldn't fulfill in this life, most likely you'll do that on the Other Side. If you've always wanted to dance and you couldn't in this life, it's certain that you are a dancer on my side and that you may have been that in many lives.

Your wants do not change on the Other Side. What you want something to be, you can construct it. This is the truest definition of synergism. On my side, you can make things become what you wish them to be. You will see people standing out in a field, beginning to construct a building simply by visualizing it. We also see people getting into debates with each other. Sometimes we even see tempers flare, and then it's over quickly. Because, you see, there's nothing to carry a grudge about. On the Other Side, nobody wants to harm anyone. The ego is not stifled.

The whole time you're down here, people are searching for who they are; yet they already *are.* There's no such thing as not being in the state of being. You are the sum total of yourself.

Did you ever ask yourself what you wanted to become? All that's required is to become an adult, live out your life, do as much good as you can, and go Home. That's all. Along the way, you may put down some flowers and stones for others to enjoy.

You make life so complicated. What religion you belong to, how many children you have, if you're married or not, whether you're old or young, whether you're fat or short or tall or thin—none of that means anything except to the person who's looking at you. It means nothing. Of course, you're supposed to take care of your body, but realize that even that is superficial.

The more you get out of yourself and don't even think about *you,* the less illness you will have. You could do all kinds of miraculous things with yourself. If you have mental pain, you can transfer it into your body. It's much more feasible to deal with that. But please pick something you can deal with, not something excruciating.

I've seen people inflict cancer upon themselves because they can't quit "eating themselves alive" over some problem, or something they hate about themselves. Cancer is *not* induced from hating another individual. It is caused from *self-hate*. That eats you up. Hating another individual can give you a terrible stomach, or kidney stones, but it will not give you cancer.

Sometime ago, Sylvia was on TV and a woman asked, "How could my daughter, a little tiny girl with cancer, ever have self-hate?"

She didn't; however, she hated too much in her past life, and she brought it over with her. Now, as many parents will tell you, the cruelest thing seems to be to lose a child. It *is* hard, but the faster they come Home, the less "soul sick" they are.

It is a most horrifying thing for anyone to lose a child, because everything in the human species has to do with survival. The fear of extinction is gigantic. So, not only are we predisposed genetically to protect ourselves from death (because we're here to learn), but so are our offspring. That is then manifested as astronomical grief and loss. We're supposed to protect at all costs. Otherwise, the human species would never have survived. There would not be any bodies for souls to come in to perfect through. This is exactly the reason why we forget about the Other Side while on Earth.

Sometimes our chart seems so clear.

That's when you're on your chart's primary track. Then at other times you go for months feeling off-track. We call it the "light" and the "dark" track, because some of your chart lines are lightly penciled in. Others, the primary lines, are a deep-blue indelible line

What is a Christian Gnostic?

Christian Gnosticism means being a seeker after your own truth and believing that everything you need to know about God can be found through intellectual reasoning. That is what Gnosticism is. That's what Jesus taught in his ministry. That's what the Society of Novus Spiritus is about.

Can our loved ones visit us after passing over to the Other Side?

They first check in to orientation, and then they come back around their loved ones; that often happens. A person will check in to the Hall of Wisdom, get everything straightened out, then come back around to visit with you.

Soul's Perfection

Be very careful of "spiritual snobbery." There is a period in your spiritual journey in which a person begins to accelerate. And in acceleration, there's a euphoria. This is all part of spiritual development, but you need to maintain a nonjudgmental attitude toward others. It does go by these stages.

When you develop spiritually, there's a marvelous feeling of euphoria. Then comes a tremendous feeling of perception, and right on the tail end of that, if you aren't careful, comes a spiritual ostentatiousness. Always be on guard for that.

Spirituality is always the master, and you're always the servant to it. After the period of ostentatiousness disappears, the perception still stays. Always the bulk of hurt resides with the person who's the most perceptive. People who are not spiritually developed don't hurt as easily nor as deeply as those who are, because of the difference in their *perception.*

As you grow spiritually, you will begin to be far more psychic than you ever imagined, because it goes hand-in-hand. You will feel and sense more. The responsibility of properly using your perception resides with you.

Don't feel that you have to incur guilt or that you have to carry around any type of karmic debt. Don't be upset with those who don't perceive as far and as wide as you do.

Now, I want you to think of your universe at this point in time, and condense it. Meditate on the fact that every single person is like a tiny universe. If you look around you, you can probably find every diverse type of personality, every life theme, and every type of heartache and rejection. If you can sustain yourself in this universe, you can do so anywhere.

We're going to talk about pivotal lives, and the factors you must work on for your perfection. This is by no means any judgment from anywhere. If you feel that you've had your hands slapped, you've missed the point. You should explore any specifics about your personality that don't make you happy; they usually link up to a past pivotal life.

Explore such things as being extroverted or introverted, giving out too much, perfectionism, living through family, excessive worry, phobic fear, fear of being alone, criticalness, thinking you're stupid, feeling sorry for yourself, obsessiveness, or being awfully nice in the sense that you're full of *awe*. Also, explore being servile, feeling guilty, any identity crisis or lack of vision about where you belong in life, indecisiveness, being too matriarchal, feeling hyperactive or insecure, or feelings of failure.

In my life, there were all of those—I was obsessive, I had an identity crisis, and I harassed others terribly. I never let anyone forget anything or have a moment's peace, even my husband. I was constantly harassing myself and everyone else about my spiritual development.

I spent 19 years living to be what seemed like 90. I was both extroverted and introverted. Going through this life with Sylvia, I've experienced much, also. So there can't really be any judgment for any entity because I'm sure that these issues will hit any one of you. More than just pinpointing aspects you're perfecting, try to realize that we all link together in the end.

You're not experiencing anything new or different from anyone else in the past, present, or future. Everyone has had a temper and has been critical, mean, and vengeful. Now, work on these things— they seem small, but they're very large because they define the essence of you. I'm convinced that you'll make great progress. The way you work on your spirituality is by gaining knowledge about it and modifying negative behaviors.

People in life can stunt your spiritual growth with kindness. If you ask someone, "How am I?" they often say, "Just fine—I think you're a really nice person." Yet they may not feel that way at all. You may have actually come into life to be a difficult person so that those around you could perfect. Fortunately, most of you are congenial most of the time.

What is a desert period?

In spiritual development, it is a very isolated period, a "crisis of faith." It's quite different from anything you've ever experienced before, but you certainly know when you're in it. It's like birth pains. Nobody has to tell a woman whether she's having them or not. During this period, you feel totally anxious and isolated from any other human being, and, worse, separate from God.

You also feel that no one has ever gone through the situation that you're going through, nor will anyone understand. You feel more than lonely—you feel totally alone. It's like walking and walking, but finding no smiles or warmth. It's as if someone has cut a hole in your solar plexus. There seems to be a void right in the pit of your stomach. During this desert period, if you're told that you're loved, it seems hard to believe.

It's almost impossible to have a life without a desert period. These times help you learn. It's a phobic, anxious, and fearful time. Don't feel deficient if you haven't gone through one. It's probably one of the most hellish states that an individual can go through because it's a displacement of reality. You don't know what's real; it's a type of psychotic episode. Psychologists have called it an *identity crisis*. It usually happens when you hit a peak that's related to a past life, in which you had decided that you'd gain and perfect.

These periods are comparable to the sophomore year of high school, which is the toughest year. This is when your theme really begins to set in, and you start to encounter obstacles to see what you are made of. It does not have to be triggered by trauma, but it can be.

"I Am"

The word *ego* is misused almost universally today. It comes from the Greek "ego," meaning "I am, I exist."

When you see someone with an overinflated "ego" structure, you really ought to say, "They have a small ego. They have no confidence within themselves."

The primary way to gain any sanction within your own God-center is to love yourself. Appreciate yourself for whatever you may be or may become. Accept yourself by knowing that you live in a world that's distorted by nonfactual things. Seek for the truth within your own soul about your own rules for living, your own way of life, and what's right for you.

Get rid of all misleading ideology and all the misguided concepts of sin. The only sins that you can commit in the whole of creation are against yourself. When you get to a point of accepting yourself totally and loving yourself unconditionally, then you're what some people call "saved." Then, of course, there is no false ego. You have a true "I am." You're the best person that you know how to be. You're not burdened by what cultures and churches have told you, such as: "You're sinful; you're bad; you're low." It's not true.

Unfortunately, you've been led to believe that religious leaders are the only ones with a direct reciprocation with God, which is terribly wrong. Every one of you can talk to God. You can do so just as simply and profoundly as any bishop, minister, or reverend. There's no stamp that our Father has given to any one person, making them better than others.

In order to survive, the ego sets up reversals and overlays. You may have had many lives or even just one in which you had to behave a certain way in order to exist. You assimilated a role. You had to sustain this overlay of behavior in order to survive the bombardment of negativity in which you've had to live.

If you haven't been able to get along in a family situation, you may have developed either introversion or arrogance. By no means is this sinful. It's possible that you're more sensitive than others, and that has caused you to assume a heavier overcoat of behavior, in order to protect your own ego structure. You wouldn't jump in ice water without anything on your body to keep you from freezing to death. You would be absolutely foolish. You have to adapt your behavior in order to sustain your ego structure.

Quit thinking of yourself as being victimized or martyred. Only when your behavior becomes a methodical, motivated, cruel, mean, deliberate, manipulated situation in order to harm someone else does it become a negative rub to you.

Many people with hard lives become very "barbed" and seem cruel because of their fear that someone will hit their vulnerability. Yet they're soft inside, much like the soft underside of a turtle, who tries not to turn over in order to survive.

Sometimes it's very kind, in the truest Christian sense, to walk up to a person and say, "I'm sorry that your life has been so hard that you hide behind cruelty." You may feel that this is not tactful, but sometimes that kind of approach cuts through the behavioral overlays. The person may feel that they must live up to this terrible image of being very embittered, because if they were to drop it, no one would know who they were anymore.

There are even some long-suffering people who have had to keep up such an image in order to satisfy others. From my side, it's amazing to watch some people actually adopt a martyr position in order to keep others around them constantly in crisis. Without them, maybe the others would not react the way they do. The martyr's role is then continually reinforced. They can't get out of it.

So we don't need to have guilt?

Guilt truly means "remorse for the intentional infringement on another's soul." This is only indigenous to the incarnate state. We don't have anything akin to guilt on my side.

The soul will evolve through different circumstances externally and internally to test and grow in spirituality. You can't rule out prior lives, which are the source of behavioral overlays. But never accept guilt if your motive is pure.

Without any negative rub in this life or any phobias or worries, you wouldn't gain any knowledge or insight. You have certain lessons to learn in life, until you finally learn acceptance of who, what, and where you are, and the relationship you have with yourself.

The True "I Am"

It is a blessing knowing that someday your life will end. It really is true. *In that, there is peace.* You *know* that you will graduate. When we come into human life, we're always so *obsessed* with, "Have I lived enough? Will I die and not complete?" The fear of death becomes overwhelming.

Yet on my side, we have it in *reverse.* The fear of *coming into life* is what is so overwhelming. Once we get to Earth, we go goofy. We forget that we have a plan and are on a mission for God.

In that time, the theme that you brought in is very important. The *companion* that you brought in along the way is very important. The *people* who are around you are important. They all add to your instinctive and creative ability to graduate and get through this life.

Especially, try to leave your "arch-enemy" behind you. I am talking about the ego. That is not the true "I am," but the part that tenaciously hangs on to the physical vehicle. It tenaciously wants, needs, and demands. It is "the child within" you that is always whining and crying. Instead of nurturing that false ego, kill it off. Put it away from you. What rises out of that is a brilliant light that shines outward instead of inward.

The false ego, which should be killed immediately, is *not* the true self. It's something like an "infection" that comes along with life.

The infection is, "I have to live; I have to have. Why can't I have?"

That "babyfied," insipid, alien infection is constantly goading us. "Am I appreciated and loved enough? Does everyone care about me enough?" It constantly has to be fed, and it becomes a dragon. That dragon turns everything dark. It's insatiable.

Say, "I will still this crying voice. Out of the silence will come the true me." The real soul can't see through or sense the infection that comes with life. It's a type of mutation when we come to this planet.

Say this every day: "I am the summation of Father God, Mother God, and my soul's perfection." In doing so, the total beauty of your soul begins to rise up. You're not so concerned about how warm you are, how full you are, how happy you are, how nurtured you are, or how much you need.

The one cry of most human beings is that they want someone in their life. So many people have a constant need for partnership. Yet these people don't realize that your life partner can sometimes be of the same sex or even a child. The *warmth* of spiritual friendships always exceeds any physical relationship.

We always think of partnerships as being the opposite sex or another *body* with us. The truest partnership that you'll ever have is your own "other side" of yourself. That's the truest form of a soulmate.

Notice how many men who are working hard for their families, and how many women who go about their business raising their families, *do not have time* for that ego voice. They are too busy caring, loving, and working toward a vision *outside* themselves. That ego voice is stilled and killed off eventually.

You're often advised to "nurture that child within." But at a certain point, you must realize that this tactic is blocking your spiritual growth. Repress it. It's one of the obstacles that came in with you. By removing the false ego that seems to be in our roots, the greatest healing in the world comes.

We have seen it in all the great leaders of the world. There were very few times when they ever turned inward to themselves. Their focus is outward to help everyone, not to simply nurture themselves.

Every day spent without giving help to one human being, in some small or large way, is a day where you have no mark on your ledger. Of course, in this life, you tend to do things in great batches. We will go for years and never do one good thing. Then we do 1,000 good things in two weeks.

People are getting to the point now where they wonder if they're doing enough good. Do *one* thing every day—that's enough. One small thing. It can be just standing at a stop sign and letting someone else proceed before you. It can be going to the bank and allowing somebody to go ahead in front of you, no matter how busy you are.

One solitary golden act puts a "gold bead" on your chart.

Your chart, of course, only applies to you. That's why all religious books have said, in some way or another, that you were building your treasure on the Other Side or heaven or whatever they called it. That's true. You *are* advancing there, but you don't know it while in life. You're taking your courses here, but the goal lies after this world.

It's very much like when Sylvia, after taking year after year of school, went to see her counselor and found out that she practically had a master's degree. All she had to do was write her thesis. She had no idea that she had accumulated so many hours. In the same way, it's so commonplace to be unaware of the credits we have accrued.. The mysteries that you have in your own soul are probably the most wondrous of all.

If your light is not shining inward on the dark side of your ego, then it will shine outward. You will be ready to serve God and fulfill the mission that's ahead of you, rather than worrying about everything.

I agree with Sylvia. She was obsessing one night about why so many people are led around by their genitalia—it's true. Of course it's wondrous that God has given us bodies that fit into one another, but why is this issue so predominant? It appeals to the ego, doesn't it?

Maybe that's why so many times in religions, people got the erroneous belief that they must go to the opposite extreme. Certainly Catholics started celibacy solely because they did not want *to support* whole families. That was absolutely a church edict. It was *not* because they wanted to be holy. It was because the church didn't want to support spouses and a whole bunch of children.

I think that some people rose to heights of celibacy purely because they realized that it reduced complications and did nothing to enhance spirituality. It seems funny that by the time most people realize this, they're too old to even care one way or the other.

If you've ever noticed, the person that you love is someone for whom you have emotional stirrings, sexual or otherwise. On the other hand, you may be repulsed by some people due to a similar chemical, "anti-sexual" reaction. Both are caused by your perception of the *beauty of the soul.*

This whole idea of coupling is beautiful. Everyone wants someone, but until you can couple with yourself—even go so far as to have a sexual union with yourself, loving the male or female side of yourself—only then will you know the true "I Am." No one can tear that apart. They can try to defame you or take things away from you, but your body—your house, your temple—will stand.

So many of you have been advanced enough to ask, "Am I on track?" The track gets all crazy and upside down when your "poor pitiful me" ego asks, "Will I be taken care of? Will I be nurtured? Will I be loved?" When that starts rising up, pluck it out. Replace it with, "Whom may I take care of? Whom may I love? Whom may I serve?" To serve His people is to serve God.

A MEDITATION TO TAKE YOU TO THE OTHER SIDE

I want to take you on a journey. Ask the archetypes and your spirit guides to surround you. Put your hands upward on your thighs in order to receive grace. Now close your eyes. I want you to surround yourself with a purple light, the royal color of spirituality, and ask that all those who have loved you and whom you have loved—from all your lifetimes, not just this one—will come around you to bless and care for you.

You are surrounded by a circle of people stacked rows upon rows—loved ones, your dear animal pets that you've loved, children that you've lost, fathers that have gone away, and husbands that you think are not there. All of them, come.

I want you to see yourself walking through a beautiful silver tube. As you walk, the most marvelous thing happens. It's almost as if the tube vibrates with millions of sparkles of light, so much so that some of you even walk faster, even skip a little bit, amazed at how with each step, these silver sparkles enter your soul and purify it.

At the end of this tunnel is a golden light in the beautiful shape of a cross. In front of you stands three golden circles that represent your total infinity, your total God Consciousness and

Father and Mother God. You make a circle with the Divinities and feel yourself part of the golden loop that is intertwined.

Now as you pass through this tube, you feel the presence of your guides on either side of you. All of a sudden, a mist hangs heavy around you. You're a little bit afraid to walk because you can't see too far ahead of you; it's much like this in life.

But then you feel warm hands on you—the love of a mother or grandmother, perhaps, who comes back. You feel them gently press you to move forward, and you're suddenly aware of a beautiful golden bridge that glimmers very faintly at first out of the mist across a beautiful rushing creek. You approach it quickly, then walk across, unafraid.

Then a beautiful meadow opens up right in front of your eyes. In the distance, you see beautiful white-maned horses frolicking, trees with fruit, and flowers on bushes growing pro- fusely everywhere.

Coming toward you are all the people who encircled you before. You feel their warm hands pulling you. You feel the warmth of this love surrounding you, and the embrace they give you. Green light seems to emanate from them toward you, which heals your entire body. Take as long as you want now, passing this green light through all parts of your body, bottom to top.

Feel your father's arms around you; feel your mother's kiss lightly on your cheek; feel your husband hold you in his arms; feel your brother come up on the other side. Speak to them.

See how familiar all of this looks. It's where you came from and where you'll go back to; this beautiful place gave birth to all humankind. It's where we all came from, the Almighty God, where I live, and where you'll come back to live.

You can't stay too long this time. But from this beautiful vision that you will carry with you, you can visit there many times. Each time you do this diligently—in mind, body, and spirit—healing will be total and complete.

Right in the middle of this field, the most important thing is a gigantic amethyst crystal. Go over and touch this purple crystal that resonates your soul. Touch it. Feel it. Ask for any message to be sent from that crystal into you.

Ask for forgiveness for yourself—not from God, but ask for you to forgive yourself. Ask for your ego to be slain like the dragon it is, and for the truest "I Am" of you to come forward. It will. In doing so, you will slay the dragons of illness and hurt and despair and grief inside you.

Feel yourself relaxed. Feel yourself inhaling the purple and green glows of those around you. Don't be sad to leave. You'll be here soon enough; even if it's 60 years from now. It is soon enough. You only came here to visit anyway.

Bring yourself back down the silver tube of light, carrying with you the emerald and amethyst lights. Bring yourself all the way out as you count to three.

Do Not Judge

Sylvia: Many of you have talked about being challenged about your beliefs within your own group. We're going to have more of that, in both our public and private domains. You must stand strong— remember, both the Hindus and the Buddhists were hacked to death when they started, just as Christians were put in the lion's den.

Everyone has to go through a trial by fire for their beliefs. Tell me honestly: In your heart, didn't you go through it to have a child? To get married? To start a new job? Those are minor issues compared to our spiritual beliefs. We have to stand firm.

I was listening to an evangelist minister one morning talking about the fact that Thanksgiving was coming, and we didn't have much to be thankful for because we were all "sinners." That's blatantly false. Did you ever, on an early morning when you had nothing to do, start clicking through channels and end up listening to these people? It's amazing.

I began to think about the word *sinners.* Let me just tell you about this minor issue, then we'll go to the big stuff. Wouldn't you lie to someone if they were dying, and you knew beyond a shadow of a doubt that they couldn't handle the truth? Or if somebody comes in wearing a garish outfit—but they're so pleased and feel so great about it—do you tell them that they look like hell? No.

Then I thought to myself, *Have I ever killed? No, not a human being*. But probably, somewhere along the line, I might have killed one's spirit without knowing it. I might have hurt someone inadvertently—but I can't take on guilt for that because I didn't mean to do it. In other words, if I really had it in my heart to hurt someone badly, then I really should have guilt.

Now, let's take this line of thought to the utmost. Let's say that someone is attacking one of my children. You better believe that without a thought—I know in my heart right now—I could pick up a gun or a knife and put them down.

Have I ever stolen? Not that I'm aware of, but if my family was starving, then you better believe that I'd steal. I would lie, cheat, and steal if it meant saving my loved ones. As always, your motive is the sole determinant of "good" or "bad" actions.

I really dread hearing people say, "I would never do such-and-such." I've stopped saying this. I don't know about you, but God has installed in me an "instant karma" button—the minute I say "I will never . . . ," I eat those words within three seconds. No delay. So let's not be smug. Let's be thankful that we're human—that we're spirit in human form, with all the attributes that God meant us to have.

At Novus Spiritus, we believe in not judging any person's soul. Through the heartaches and trials of life, people gain knowledge. Even so, who has not had thoughts of vengeance? We're so afraid, aren't we, to wish that someone would drop dead and leave us alone. As if we were that powerful.

I heard somebody say the other day, "I'm trying to buy a new house. Let's not talk about it now so we don't jinx it." I said, "What? Is God going to say, 'Listen, I heard that; now I'll stop it'"?

When we graduate from this planet, we can prance all over the place. Only the bravest come here, because it's the insane asylum of the universe. Now, you don't have to believe me, but just look around as you go about your daily life. You'll see that I'm telling you the God's truth.

We need to form a unit of strength, of power, and of thanksgiving. Do not force yourself to feel thankful for everything. Just say, "I'm thankful that I came in at a time when I could effect a change through my beliefs."

Those who don't stand with you—let them go. You have a lot of high roads to cover.

We have a long journey, but I promise you that it will never be boring. It may be silly, it may be fun, it may even be tragic, but it will never be boring. Boredom is a real killer. My grandmother asked me one time, "What's the matter with you?" I was young, and I said, "I'm bored." And she replied, "Only stupid people get bored." I only said that once. Do you know that to this day if I'm bored, I will never say it? I get bored a lot, but I say, "I'm restless." If you're really intelligent, you can always find something to do. Be thankful that you found your spirituality. You haven't arrived yet, but you sure are on the right track.

I remember the day that Francine *told* me that I was going to start a religion. She asked me when I was going to get busy and open the doors. Novus was about a year old when she said, "This religion makes God stretch. It makes Him smile." That was enough for me. God is no longer cramped by the dogma man puts on Him.

Wouldn't you hate for someone to speak for you? People do this to me all the time, which is unfair. Wouldn't you hate for someone to always quote you and speak for you?

We let Mother and Father God speak for Themselves, because They are love. Love speaks continuously with forgiveness and grace. It does not start with "You will follow these rules . . ."

Moses came down off the mountain with a big list of rules. I think that Moses wrote them when he was up there. I have nothing to prove that, but I believe it with all my heart. Consider how long he was gone. Now, since God is all-perfect and powerful, couldn't He write the Commandments instantly? Moses did it to control his people. Of course, everyone innately knows you do not steal, murder, or bear false witness. But the Ten Commandments were the first of many "do nots" used to control the masses.

There is an old friend of mine named Warren whom I dated when we were teenagers in Kansas City, Missouri. Over the years, we've kept track of each other. I called him on his birthday not too long ago to chat. It had been maybe 12 years since we'd talked. He said he'd recently been sitting around in a meeting, and my name came up. They wanted to know why I'd started a religion.

He told them, "Well, Sylvia and I go back a long way. Let me tell you a story. We were 15 years old, and we were walking through Gillum Park in Kansas City." He told them we'd been talking about the fact that he didn't believe in God, and I went into a full-blown rage. (I know you can't believe that *I* would do that.)

I said to him at the time, "That's ridiculous and stupid. You've got to," and on and on I went about God. "Everything good in this world comes from God in Heaven." I had my hands out as I usually do, and *a bird pooped in my hand.* Both Warren and I felt that our positions had been justified.

But the point is that he said, "I'm surprised that, considering the fervor you had to make the truth known, you didn't start a religion many years ago." It took terrible courage to profess to the world that I'm a psychic, and I think it took twice as much courage to start a religion.

Our faith in ourselves is tested constantly. Ultimately, it's a test of our faith in God, although we never see it that way. A Novus minister asked me one morning, "Why is it so easy when we're here together in church, yet so hard when we go outside?" We come together on Sundays and we plug in to charge our spiritual battery; then we can go out and fight the daily battles. People tend to spend their whole lives with familiar and well-known "sins" and "demons." You know why? They're comfortable. They're predictable and repetitive, therefore known to us, whereas the unknown is more frightening.

We say, "Oh, well, I'm following the rules. I suffer, feel unworthy, bow my head, and genuflect because God is ominous and fearful."

Not our God. Not the God-center inside each of us. So to break the pattern, you've got to audit yourself. We do this for everything else. We read books to improve absolutely everything, then pass the books to all our friends. We don't realize that success means not repeating those circles of pain. You will always have a circle, but find a circle that has less darkness in it.

If your spouse is mean today, perhaps he or she will be meaner tomorrow and next week. But you decide to stay with this person because it's something you know. You have to decide how much misery you can stand. Does that mean that we should give up all our old circles? No, but we can put them away from us.

Evil begets evil. Violence begets violence. Negativity begets negativity. So put it away from you. Do not give energy to it.

"I have to hold on to this," you say, "because this holds me up. This is something I need in front of me." That's what life seems to be. Props. They're just props. The span of a lifetime, compared to eternity, is a blink of an eye. Have you ever thought about how wonderful that is?

It's also inspiring to come to the knowledge that you need nothing. Having nothing that ties you makes you so free. The more you know, the less you need, as the aborigines say.

I always used to be so concerned that I would lose things; I believed that I had to keep the things I'd worked so hard for. Then all of a sudden one day, I just let go of it. I was so happy. I'm not identified by my house or car, or even by my ministers or my sons.

I am identified by myself!

You must identify your God-center by yourself. Then open your hands and let it go. Until you, truthfully, in your own mind, let go of all the pain and suffering—all the things that are tied to you—you can never be free and well. Even when you acquire something, it's only temporary. You have to open your hands and let it go with a blessing. Be like a parent watching over your children until they grow up—then you let them go. Do not keep repeating the old circles.

Things that are freer fly back to you. If they do not, and you have nothing to support you, then you have yourself. That's the name of the game. God wants us here to experience for Him. We are the fingers of God that move in this world.

So often, our parishioners tell me, "Here in your church, I feel that I've come home." I hear that constantly. It means more to me than I can express. You should see the letters I get telling me how people have been healed and helped, which just fills my soul with gratitude to God. It must go on. Of course, it will.

I think for so long people thought, *It will get too tough for those Gnostics, and they will just throw up their hands.* If you know me, then you know this: I will never give up. Not until they carry me out feet first, and then the ministers will carry on afterwards.

My grandmother used to say to me, "Within your weakness lies your strength, sleeping." Don't ever give up. All things come to those who believe and wait. Trust me. I'm a living example of that. Those of you who can't wait, you give up too easily. You then lose everything.

Church should be a community, a body of people moving together to help each other morally, mentally, physically, spiritually, and financially if we can. My church, Novus Spiritus, hardly ever talks about money. I don't even believe in tithing. In fact, our policy has always been that if you don't have any money when the donation box comes around, you take some out. I have wonderful people who cannot give an offering, but do you know what they do? They offer us their talents, their writing or printing ability. That's what it's all about. If you can't do anything else, then I will give you a service, and you can bring me a bag of potatoes. The world is going to be like that. Believe me when I tell you. There will be a trade system.

Every day in every way, surround yourself more and more strongly with white, purple, and gold lights.

When it gets really tough, open up your hands. Have you ever noticed that we clench our fists a lot? Open up your hands and say, "It is all for you, God—all for the greater good through which I'm living." *You* are the God Consciousness. Unless you go through *you,* you're never going to find God.

MEDITATION TO KNOW GOD

I want you to see or sense a total immersion. You are breathing it in. You sense a total and complete unity with Mother God, Father God, and your own God-center. Meditate on Mother God, the feminine principle, ruling this planet. We pay homage to Her strength, fairness, and joy. Next, think of Father God, who is the intellectual principle, the seat of the "I Am." Now envision the God Consciousness within you, as Jesus wanted it to be in order for you to experience the whole Gnostic faith and your search for truth.

The pink light that suffuses all around us begins to intertwine and take care of all our loved ones—our children, our family, our parents. We ask for shafts of green light now to shoot through every one of them and anyone who is ailing, bringing them joy, peace, and healing of mind, body, and spirit. Let the circle get bigger and bigger. Pray that you ascend to God and that your absolute knowledge—not faith—gets stronger, knowing that God is the key.

You do not just hope He is there—you know it. The Holy Spirit, the love between Father and Mother God, is radiated to all of us. This is the power of the Trinity that shines upon us. It is seated within and around us. Feel the power that exudes from each and every one of us like golden threads linking us together, getting us through our difficulties. We are each wires that can be plugged in to God to receive grace.

Say within your heart now, "It is all for you, God. I give it all to you." The will of God is no different from our will. It is the same.

We ask this in the name of the Mother, the Father, the son, the Holy Spirit, and the God Consciousness in all of us: Bear us up, cleanse us, give us hope, give us the truth, and give us infused psychic knowledge about which path to take.

Bring yourself up, feeling absolutely marvelous.

Appreciation

I hear all the time in the reading room, "Sylvia, I find no gratitude or appreciation from people. This is such a thankless life." And I say to them, "Yes, that's true."

However, it's true on one level, but untrue on another. When we came into this life with our chart, we agreed that we would come down here to experience life for Almighty God, Who, in His total knowledge and static intelligence, cannot experience it. We are the experiencing parts of God.

When we came here from the Other Side, not one of us said, "Will I be appreciated for this? Will I get gratitude or any kind of compensation?" There was no guarantee.

On the Other Side, we're not interested in such things, but this world brainwashes us. We come to believe that we "should" have a certain hair color, weight, height, home, and number of kids and cars. We are "supposed" to rise high on the ladder of success.

We collect people around us who brainwash us and tell us what to do. They can be mothers, fathers, sisters, brothers, family, and other people. My mother used to say to my sister and me, "Sylvia will be the one who stays home and has all the babies, and Sharon will be the career girl." How very wrong she was.

But from this moment on, please write across your immortal soul: "My choices will come from me. They come from within." What was originally written on your soul was appreciation, gratitude, remuneration, and grace from God. Now, this doesn't mean that you have to live your life without ever getting thanks and recognition, but don't live your life with this expectation. You know why? My husband, Larry, says it best: "Life will have its way with you."

We toil in dark corners. We give up our lives for things. We take roads that we don't necessarily want because of our children, or for someone's love, or a church, or for those we care about. But please stop grumbling about it.

If you're going down a side road instead of the main highway, say, "Well, look. The scenery is nice here, too." If you get in a thorn-bush, you could say, "Well, this is a new experience," instead of griping about it. What appreciation do you have for yourself since you decided to come down here? *There* is the appreciation and the reward you should have for yourself. Say, "Good for me. I'm going to give myself an accolade, and I'm grateful to myself that I could even make it through."

Some years ago when my life was very hard and my world was

crumbling, I just got up every day and simply moved and survived. I put everything aside except my church and the people I loved. I couldn't have made it if not for that external focus.

Then when I got through it, I said to myself, not in a conceited way, "Wow, you did it." I didn't care if anybody else was proud. *I* was proud that I survived. A lot of people said, "You will never make it through this. Nobody has, really." That made me mad. Anger is a great motivator. I said, "You think I'm done? I'll show you."

In every life, you get slammed this way and that, and sometimes the hardest slams can come from your own home, can't they? Those can really get you. Our beloved God above knows what He is doing, and She knows what She is doing. *You* know what you're doing, ultimately. Don't give up.

There is another phenomenon. Let's call it "superstition," which abounds in this world, even to this day. I have to tell you the truth—if somebody spills salt, I throw it over my left shoulder. I don't know why. My grandmother and everybody always did it, so I just do it. I've actually watched a salt shaker lying on its side spilling out, and thought, *I won't do it this time,* but I do it anyway.

How many of you can say, "Everything I ever wanted came easily"? Everything *I* have ever wanted in my life was hard. Yet, in our gut, in our heart, the God Consciousness, there is a message from God that says, "Keep on keeping on."

Once in a while, just to keep us here, there's a little dollop of grace dropped upon us, isn't there? You feel so lucky for winning the plant on the table at a luncheon. That's the kind of thing I get—"Hurrah, I'm holding the winning raffle ticket. I get the poinsettia. Aren't I a lucky girl?" They are very little dollops, aren't they? But you won it, and it's yours.

Never give up and say, "Oh, it's too hard to grow spiritually. I'm just fine the way I am." That's stupid. Even though things are hard, you still have to go through them. Fight for the things you want. Otherwise, we would all just sit around like blobs. No.

When you clutch the hand of Mother and Father God, say, "Hey, walk with me." They are your friends. Do not visualize Them way up above. They are here. Hold on to Them. And if They don't walk fast enough, then yank Them: "Get over here. Listen to me."

Sometimes this is how we have to be with God: "I'm going to yell so loud that You are going to pay attention." God always pays attention. But when *your* soul pays attention, you elevate to God. Then God can activate. Open your heart to the God Consciousness. Don't be afraid.

One of my ministers said to me, "Sylvia, it's so hard to be positive." You bet it is. Anybody who tells you otherwise is an idiot. It's tough to be here because of what we see going on in the world, and it's not getting any better.

But we're going to be positive through all the negativity, because that's the path for gaining higher spirituality.

Meditation of Light

Ask for the God Consciousness to come and descend upon you. Put your hands upward on your thighs, and keep the white light of the precious Holy Spirit around you—it is Mother and Father God's love for each other, which descends upon you in a bubble of light.

Make this light so brilliant that it not only extends around you, but swirls out and encompasses your loved ones, your family, and all the people in the world who need help. From your light, the power that you can call on from God spills out and encompasses all the animals, children, and people who are sick.

Then, bring a green light through your own body to make you healthy and strong. Extend it out now to all your loved ones here and on the Other Side. Ask those who have passed to attend to you today and to stand behind you with the archangels, the archetypes, and your spirit guides.

Keep us, God, from addictions. Keep us from harm and hurt. Dear God, bless our days. Take away the pain. Ease our minds, oh God. Lighten our burdens and our thoughts. Keep our motives pure. Let me have the ability, dear God, to heal myself and others.

Let me be strong to the very end. And when the end comes, let me go quickly, with dignity and without pain, God, so I can stand before You with shining eyes, and You can see directly into my heart, free of all wrongs—even of the human foibles.

Feel the grace of God enter your soul, heart, and mind. Feel the energy come into you directly from God. Feel yourself going right into the heart of God. Feel that blessed peace at the reunion; feel your homesickness vanish. We are back with our Creator.

Carry this peace and love with you. Give it out as if you carry a gigantic basket of love and spirituality. Profusely sprinkle it among all whom you love.

Feel the energy coming right up through the very bottoms of your feet—up through your feet, your ankles, your calves, your knees, your thighs, and the buttocks area. All through the trunk. Down through the shoulders, the upper arms, the lower arms, the hands, the fingertips. Around the face, the mouth, the nose, the eyes, the forehead.

On the count of three, come all the way up feeling absolutely marvelous, better than you have ever felt before. One, two . . . three.

Anvil or Hammer

Edwin Markham, a U.S. poet, said, "When you are the anvil, bear—if you are the hammer, strike." An anvil is a long metal object upon which hot iron metal is beaten into various forms. The anvil just stands, but the hammer is what beats the molten lump of iron into a useful form.

Some of us are anvils, and some are hammers. Through our lives, there are big sections in which we have to switch roles. Many times, we *do not want to do either one.* We do not want to take or give the beating, do we?

Here's the amazing thing. We always think, when we're being the anvil or the hammer, that we're doing it for ourselves. And yes, that's part of it. But there's another part that you should know: Everyone on the Other Side watches your life and your mission. They learn from it and absorb your experience along with you.

What do you do when you prepare for battle? You become trained, you research, and listen to your leaders. The general stands in front of you and says, "This type of tactic was used in Desert Storm, and this at Waterloo."

Every life is a battle, whether it's large or small. It's fought on some battlefield. Everything is relative to *you*. How many battles have you fought in your life? Was it useless? No.

You may have said, "Well, who knows what I'm going through?" Those on the Other Side watch and learn. The Council says, "Look at how strong they are. Now, can't you do the same?" Who knows how many souls fan out from your experience and go and make a good fight against the dark?

You will live and die in this world—and never think it's for naught. What does this world mean, really? Will you live on in legend? In infamy? What does that matter? What matters is what God knows of your soul, and how much you walk in God Consciousness.

When you get to the Other Side, you will look back and be proud that you were strong in your life. You survived. You raised children. You supported your loved ones with their problems. You made it. You lived each day for God, seeking your own truth.

So think, today: Are you an anvil, or are you a hammer? Know when to be still and solid, but also know when to strike. Do not sit in pain if you can activate. Move out, do something, walk forward.

There is nothing more precious than your freedom to love God and to worship as you see fit. If you lose that, regardless of where you are, you've lost the truth to yourself. That's what Gnosticism is about. Be true to yourself, whatever that may be.

At times, we must be warriors—we must be the hammer that strikes and strikes. There's nothing worse than apathy. The only thing that comes close is despair. These two emotions can bring about such evil in your life.

Fight the thought, "I'm going to sit and wait and see." No, not even in your own life. You must now be a warrior, a hammer, for God and for yourself. Put the armor on. That armor means, "I am for truth and light and God consciousness. I want to rid the world of guilt and pain and suffering."

Is that unrealistic? Probably, judging by my life, but then, let's think about this: What is reality? Reality is synergistically what we make it. It's our truth before God, which we're following in the light, in the path of Jesus and Buddha and Mohammed. That's a proven path from ancient writings. So think today, in your own life, do you want to be the hammer that molds something, or do you want to be the anvil that sits? It's all right either way, but when you're sitting, be strong. Be solid iron, not a jellyfish.

Every single soul adds to the experiencing part of God, which contains everything. So if you try to please people only *on this* plane, you're missing the point. We are experiencing and marking our souls with the white light for the *Other Side* to witness. They are the ones we should please. Realize that many people witness your actions. Do you now feel like you're being microscopically viewed? Well, you are. There's no doubt about that. Should this make you feel self-conscious? No. It should make you feel *proud,* because a lot of souls are too afraid to come down here.

Here is the way churches really started out. They said, "Come and give witness to what you believe." They didn't say, "If you don't come, God is going to send you straight to hell." That's crazy. It was originally simply to give witness to what you believed.

If you don't witness your truth, then a whole part of your life has fallen short. Witness what you believe—whatever it may be—in your own life, in your families and job, and in your spirituality. Stand up and witness your truth. If something is wrong, stand up and be heard. Now when you do, you may get slapped a little bit or even a lot. But in the long run, isn't it marvelous to know that no matter what "slings and arrows of outrageous fortune" are inflicted upon us, we can still stand?

Be the hammer now, if you feel you should, and strike. Strike for your own justice, your own peace. Find a place where you can have peace in your own heart. Perhaps someone is causing you pain. Then move away. There's nothing else to be accomplished by taking continual abuse. Sometimes you can't move away from it, but often we stay on too long, don't we? We keep feeling that we can "fix" it. Sometimes you can't. Some have a fear of being alone. We're all alone, although we rarely stop and think about it. We can link arms, hands, and bodies, but we're alone. When we go back Home, we can merge and be close and happy. There's a long road to this life, and a lot of fun to be had. It just takes a while to find someone worthy of your love.

The test of individuals is how much pain they can withstand, and how much strength comes through at their weakest point. Sometimes strength means just moving—just getting up and moving forward, mindless as that may seem.

Be imbued with the fire of the Holy Spirit and your own convictions about life. Pull it into you. The fire you will feel will be a growing, constant, spiritual questioning; a love of God; and the feeling that you have fulfilled your contract. You will do good, hurt no one, and then go Home.

HEALING MEDITATION

Put your hands upward on your thighs, and surround yourself today with emerald-green light. It begins to expand, coming directly from the hearts of Mother and Father God. Wonderful shards of green seem to break off from their aura and come directly into your heart and soul.

You feel the love of Father and Mother God, and the Holy Spirit surrounds you. Ask that the spirit of God come in, healing and washing away all pain.

Move this green light out so far that you ask for the Holy Spirit to carry it through to the hearts and minds of people who are cruel, prejudiced, unforgiving, or vengeful. Ask that no one in the world sees skin color anymore.

We ask that the homeless find homes; that there be a cure for AIDS; that people will not suffer so excruciatingly in the silence of their own hearts; and that there is a healing mentally, physically, and spiritually.

May every heart become a soft little drum that, beating, begins to say, "Let's be rid of the dogma and fear and control." We pray for that. The drum gets louder. My drum has always been very loud. Today I pass my drum to you. Hear the cadence. Let's line up and march with the sense of wellness, releasing all past-life resonances, all pain and suffering. All the wrongs we think we did, or we might have done—let them go today.

Behind this emerald-green light that heals stands Mother and Father God. Now they're embracing us. Ask them to intercede and take away the pain, sorrow, suffering, and injustice. Set your soul free.

Wrap all your pain—body, mind, and soul—into a ball, hand it to God, and watch it dissolve. Feel the relief. The air you exhale is releasing all the dark smoke in the body.

Ask that someday you will be a spiritual beacon of light in the lonely desert that is this world. May we bring peace today. We pray in our hearts for the health and strength of the animals and children who are being hurt. With the strength of one will, we could do it—and we have the indomitable wills of many. Who knows what little shard of light will reach somebody somewhere and enlighten their soul.

Take a deep breath and let it all go. Begin to bring yourself up, keeping this brilliant emerald light around you along with the white light. Bring yourself all the way up to consciousness, on the count of three. One, two, THREE . . .

---

[1] See Book 1 in Sylvia's JOURNEY OF THE SOUL series: *God, Creation, and Tools for Life*, Hay House, 1999.

§ Chapter Two ℰ

KARMA AND DHARMA

Sylvia: *Karma* is a strange word. No matter how many times I go on TV, no matter how many times I talk about this issue, people are still convinced that karma is something they're working through with another person. No—you're working through your *own* karma, which means your *own* experience.

I asked Francine, "Why did I begin a church?" Well, it was to help us stay on-track. If we're around negativity all the time, we have nothing else to recharge our spiritual battery with. To me, our church is more important, fulfilling, and enlightening than any "fear trap," because it's positive and gives grace. All of us are out there all week long, dealing with people, driving in traffic, having our egos bruised to pieces, worrying about ourselves and everyone else. There's nowhere we can go to take off those overlays of behavior that we carry, and find love and grace.

Grace and karma are both considered mystical. What is grace? It's getting in touch with your God-center. But we can't always do that ourselves. When we came down into this life, we came down with a theme and a purpose. There are many life themes—some examples are Tolerance, Warrior, Catalyst, Pawn, Humanitarian, and Loner. We keep one theme throughout our whole lives. Experiencing for our own soul, we will write in any number of negatives for ourselves. So, we overcome obstacles to gain as many "A's" as possible on the report card for our theme.

But since we're separate from the God and the Holy Spirit, we *do* get off-track sometimes. That doesn't mean we're going to lose our immortal soul, but it makes life tougher. One of my ministers said to me, "Every test now is a lesson to be learned. I know I'm going to learn it and pass it, because it's so much easier with this knowledge."

Stop thinking about yourself. Stop worrying. Let God handle that. "Thy will be done" is probably one of the hardest things to truly live by. When considering that phrase, it's easy to say, "Wait a minute . . . maybe His will is not mine." What are you talking about? It's got to be, because your will and His are the same. You are a part of Him.

Karma only means that you're experiencing for your own soul's development. You're not bound to anything else in this life. That doesn't mean that we don't love and give to others. If we don't, then we're having the wrong type of karmic experience.

Be rational. If you were meant to be alone, you would not have hands that reach, a mouth that kisses, eyes that see, and a body that fits into another's. You would not be able to speak, because there would be no reason for communication.

However, the only person that you have to rely on for soul experience is *you*. You can't do that without grace and love. You weren't meant to. Certainly, life is negative. Didn't Jesus show us that it was? But that doesn't mean we can't get through it with grace, love, and humor.

So we must get rid of the guilt, hellfire, damnation, and all the other silliness that has kept people under control. True religion has got to grow and be a bastion for help, love, and giving. It's got to be a temple, a home for the aged, a place for children. It's got to be the way that Christianity was meant to be—the way Jesus meant it to be—without the threat of hellfire and damnation. We've got to end this rotation of lives.

Those of you who want to come back into life—although I think you're crazy—you can, of course. Most of the people I'm seeing don't want to come back. They want to finish, go to the Other Side, and have a great time. As one of my ministers said, "All you have to do is go to the gazebo (or anywhere in meditation), make your mind quiet, and ask for the first message that comes in."

Ask a question. Wait for the first message that comes in. And please rule out the word *imagination*. That's probably the worst word ever coined. You cannot imagine something that was never there. Imagery is part of your mind. It's real.

Everyone can get in contact with their spirit guide. As Francine said, "We're all waiting here to tune in the right station." You may have been told that you're not worthy enough to reach God. Of course you are.

God does not play favorites. Quit making Him humanized. God does not have pettiness, jealousy, meanness, crankiness, or peevishness. He's omnipotently perfect. We're evolving toward our own perfection for God.

My religion never carries any hellfire and brimstone, but it does impart a heavy load because it puts our own load back on us. People don't like that. They would rather blame their life on some nebulous god, or on "karma" or "my theme."

You are the one who is doing it to yourself. That's reassuring, because it means that the power is wholly within you. God did not send you down here; rather, you *chose* to come. You made a contract with God to come down and experience for Him. And within you, if you just open up, are all the tenets and beliefs and all the faculties you need. Open up the top of your head and let it come through.

Did you ever see pictures of monks who had shaved the tops of their heads? The resulting ring of hair is called a *tonsure*. The reason for it is to let God's infusion of knowledge come in. Now, you need not shave your head, but *do* open your mind to God and knowledge.

Please love yourself as God loves you. What does it matter if somebody gives you a slight one day? Are you going to remember it in ten years? Do not judge the person, only the act.

You don't need to be overly placid or humble, either. I don't want you wimping around—if somebody does something to you, speak up. Have dignity. If somebody hurts you, show righteous anger. That doesn't mean you should be militant, however.

Don't let people walk on you, because you're carrying a spark of the Divine. When somebody hurts you, speak up and tell them that it hurt. If somebody aggravated you, tell them that. You may find out that you are aggravating as well, but that's all right, too.

Karmic Hammer

The word *karma* has been bantered around and misused so much that I'm sure everyone has become confused. Too often it is misunderstood to be some tremendous backlash—some kind of wrath from the "Great Beyond" or whatever.

This misconception has made people almost as repressed as those I call the "judgmentalists." It makes you "fear based" rather than spiritually based. Every emotion such as anger, vengeance, or hurt seems sure to carry with it a karmic barb, but that's not true.

Now, in the original texts, the concept of karma had nothing to do with judgment. There was no God sitting around judging. How could He be, when He is omnipotent, holding and loving you just as Mother God does?

When you first came down into life, you said, as all of us did, "I cannot test my soul in a perfect environment. I'm going "down the chute" to learn. I'm going away to boot camp; I'm going down to Earth."

We decided on our theme, whether it was Tolerance, Experience, or Humanitarian, with our little option line heading for the test. [The option line refers to one area of your life that you have not clearly defined in your chart; it is left open.] We reincarnate; this must be so. It's not logical that a loving God lets a darling baby be run over by a truck in the middle of the street. Why should someone who has done good all their lives end up all crippled and bent? Why should someone who has been cruel and mean rise above the heights of everything?

In the future, we're going to see more and more "instant karma" occur. In other words, when victimized in a deliberately hostile and premeditated way, people will snap back. The good things that we've done will come forward, but not without trial. If you really want to learn about separating the chaff from the wheat, get a trauma in your life.

Some people have a superstition that if they get too close to others, they're going to "catch" their problems. It's like, "If you're going bankrupt or getting divorced and I'm around you, maybe I'll get it." As a result of this thinking, we miss the times to increase our own good karma by helping someone in need. I have. You have by even reading this far. We're bucking a society that doesn't understand. More and more will join in.

Stop using "karma" as a hammer over your own head. I've heard people say, "I can't leave my husband even though he beats me and the kids, because it's my karma." Such a person may, in actuality, be karmically destined to grow through the experience of pushing that abusive person out of her life. God did not mean for anyone to come down here to suffer endlessly.

Now, you have to ask yourself, "Am I creating my own problems, or is it outside of myself? Are the external things really that bad, or am I pulling them inside of me?" Review your life. Is it really that bad? Are you really so sick that you can't pull yourself up again? Is it really so horrendous that you can't go on? Is there no one in this world who loves you? Are you going to end up living on the street? No. It is the inner cry of the soul.

I will live and die and believe that a human being can come forward and love their God for the sake of love. Because I am a parent and you have been parents in other lives, could you tolerate it if your child only comes forward to love you out of fear? How horrendous is that! Do you know what a priest told me years ago when I asked him about that? He said, "Well, I'm sure that God would prefer that. But human beings, the way they are, can't do that." Hearing this, I was screaming inside my head because it's wrong.

I love God because He is there, omnipotent and good. What you need to be afraid of is yourself. "It is what *you* in human form do *to yourself* that works you over," as Francine says.

The "poor me" routine is good for about an hour and a half, and then how good is it? What's so important, anyway? "I have nobody in my life," you may say. "I don't have Mr. or Ms. Right." But if you've opened that door once, you can do it again.

Do you realize that there's no perfect right one for you? I don't care how wonderful the person is—there isn't. Nobody gives you a guarantee that it would be fair or that you'd be happy. Do you always think, as I once did, that good guys finish first? No, they don't. However, we can take comfort because evil does get punished—not immediately, but at some point. That's really what karma is all about.

It's not difficult to truly understand karma. When you embrace it, your whole soul fills up with spirituality. You understand, then, that this is only a transient place. Then how much do the cares and woes of today matter?

Francine and my grandmother always said, "Who will care 100 years from now?" Do you think our petty problems will be remembered? Does it matter if we will be remembered for anything? We're just cogs in a wheel that spins endlessly. Wouldn't you rather be in something that you knew spreads good and love and warmth? Isn't that an eternal mission, better than living with fear, sin, and debasement of the very part of you that is God?

How dare anyone attempt to destroy your estimation of the individual soul within you? Then they tell you that it's "constructive criticism." We must love the soul—personality is another matter. It's an overcoat that we wear.

However, I do know people whose personality will hopefully change before they get to the Other Side. And I won't like them there either. Some people whom I've met simply have something very wrong with them, the essence of which is very deep. I don't care what they do on the Other Side—they're just not going to be any better. Francine says they do eventually, but they have to go through many lives. Good. Then they won't be there when I am.

You have to allow yourself to dislike certain things. That's human. Never keep that kind of stuff in. It causes cancer. Those are normal emotions; there's a reason we have hate. You're meant to get through that so that you can give and receive love. I still know people who are convinced that they stay down here because they're being cursed and they have karma to work off. Please, please, stop. Never let people say that to you. Stop them—clean it up!

This "New Age" of religion, the new way of everything—why do you suppose it got started? People are sick and tired of being bamboozled and criticized by people who say one thing and live another. That's why everybody went on a search.

We allowed ourselves, our souls, to be given over to people whom we thought we could trust. But they never researched for themselves. Gnostics, on the other hand, are researchers. We say, "Oh, really? Is that true? Let's research and find the source. Let's go to the Dead Sea Scrolls, the Nag Hammadi, the early teachings, the writings of the Essenes, and the early gospels that are omitted from the Bible."

Go, read, and stand fully in the light. Know that you are with the truth of what Jesus believed. Know in your heart that you are the Truth and the Way and the Light.

Experience

People use karma as an excuse. You *can't* say that you live with someone awful because it's your karma. You don't have to put up with a rotten kid or mean in-laws or an unsatisfying job, marriage, health, or anything because of karma.

The one obligation that you do have, karmically, is to *finish* whatever you begin. Let me tell you how you must finish your own karma. Say, hypothetically, that you start a relationship—either a romance or a friendship—and you are the major instigator behind it. Then somewhere along the line you outgrow the relationship, or it outgrows you, or whatever. Your karmic obligation, unfortunately, says that you must be the one to go in, face the relationship, and end it. This principle is the same with jobs or anything else.

So many times when we get into bad situations or money problems, we sit and hope that someone will come along and help us, right? We think that if we just wait long enough or stall long enough, then something will happen. On occasion, for some people, a "white knight" does appear to give a hand. But most of the time, you are the one who has to face the music and finish out the situation.

You must say, "I can't spend any more money," or something similar. Then proceed from there. Otherwise, our lives become too tied up in long, drawn-out situations. This can even occur with our children. Now, how do you end a relationship with children? You never really *end* it with your children, but what you have to do is stop the karmic tie. In other words, you started it with your pregnancy—you wanted the child. Therefore, at some point, you must release the karmic obligation to the child. Karma means, in this case, that awful tearing feeling where you are painfully tied to the child.

I want you to think today about who in your life is really causing you pain. Who is it? Why are you perpetuating this relationship? Is the person related to you? With children, you can't really get rid of them, especially if you're like me. But what I did, because I had a tremendous karmic tie with my youngest son, was to finally release him. It wasn't because we were causing each other pain, but we were so closely connected that everything that hurt him also hurt me, and vice versa. I finally had to say, "Please, please, in the name of God, you must start wending your way out of my life—not just physically, but mentally, so that both of us can get peace from this."

Francine always told me this, which I think is absolutely marvelous: "To honor your father and your mother is fine, but only if they are honorable." Do you know how wondrous that is? Do you know what a load that takes off of you? If you had your parents living right down the street, would you choose them for friends? Many times you wouldn't. As we get older, we *can* choose. If we have a lousy mother, we become a better mother as a result. And so we're grateful to her, because through her we learned what *not* to do. So these negative things can become wondrous. No one knows whether they're a good mother or a good wife. The only proof is in the outcome of things. It depends on how satisfied you are with it, and how much you've given.

I want to mother everybody, take care of them, give them chicken soup or matzo balls. Many of us are like this. Francine said, "As the New Age dawns upon us, more of us will want to help other people." Listen to your own soul, and note how many times you think, *How can I help more? How can I do more for others?* Then do it.

It's beginning to spread now more than ever in the history of the world. There's a restlessness within the soul. We've seen the passing of another millennium, and all around us people tell of the karma they've created in themselves and in this very earth.

We're going to stop the negative karma of guilt, sin, and fear. We *must* put a stop to it.

I really recommend that you see a movie, even though it's laborious and tedious, called *The Last Temptation of Christ*. There are some great lines, especially when St. Paul meets Jesus during the dream sequence. Jesus comes up to St. Paul, who's screaming and yelling about the fact that Jesus died for our sins and is resurrected and that Jesus had made a deal with the devil, which he did not realize.

Jesus says to Paul, "I did not die on the cross. Look, I'm still living." Paul turns to him and says, "If I want you to be the crucified Christ, *you will be.*"

It was all a P.R. thing, but it really doesn't matter. True Christianity doesn't depend on whether Jesus was crucified. But down through the ages, and certainly today, Christianity has been based on the fact that Jesus *had to be* sacrificed.

That's wrong. The God Consciousness within us will go on experiencing life without the crucifixion. That state of mind is based on who Jesus was *when he lived as a man.*

The whole idea of guilt has always been, "You *must* suffer and be miserable and unhappy." This is a "veil of tears," a "valley of death." It's no picnic, is it? If anybody says it is, then I worry very seriously about their sanity.

The more advanced you become spiritually, the more you have independent notions and ideas and beliefs. The more farseeing you are, the more it hurts. Awareness does not bring with it a barrel of laughs. It brings with it hardships and hurt. While we're spiritually advancing and becoming more aware, our antennae go out: We become more psychic, more intuitive, and more feeling.

That is its own price to be paid, isn't it? You can't reach a spiritual level without being psychic. The two are absolute. There are very few things in this life that are absolute. But the more you love God and the more you try to follow what's going on in this life, the more it comes totally to your consciousness that you're absolutely a spiritual entity and must experience the pain of life.

The main thing we have to realize about relationships is that there's a coupling. We like to be two-by-two, but there are some of us who can't be. Some are loners. But in all of life, there is a coupling with a friend and with your God-center. But to have another entity in your life—that's what it's really about.

Please, when you read this, use your own judgment. Take what you want and leave the rest. People sometimes believe anything instead of relying on their own God-center to direct them. I can only give you a broad overview. I can't point to you and say, "You must do exactly as I say by these rules."

I can't experience your God-center. I may know it's there, but it is individual. Your karmic life experience is totally different from mine. That's what makes us so alone—don't you see that it's for God? As each one of us touches, smells, feels, and senses, our souls rise and the emotion lets loose at certain points. Every one of those things is a karmic experience. If you cut your finger, that's an experience, too. But another person will go through the same experience in a totally different way. Do you know what we spend most of our lives looking for? We say, "Please, does someone know how I feel?" Our whole lives are spent searching for love, even more than material happiness. In readings, people want to know about their finances and health, but more important, they ask, "Who can I love, and who loves me?" That is the thing that will always make the world go around.

As we search for love, we are always asking our partner, "Do you experience as I do?" Once in a while, the person says yes. But how many times can we confess to a person the dark thoughts we have? We think, *No one's had these thoughts; no one's had the same panic or anxieties; no one's ever loved their child or spouse like I have.*

Yes, they have. Not uniquely like you—no. No one can ever be uniquely like you. There is only one of you in the whole universe. Your experience and your karma are different from anybody else's. But you make a circle. And once you've completed the circle, then *close it off.*

When things begin to seem too synchronistic, you say, "Wait a minute. I've done this before, haven't I? Isn't this new guy the same guy I divorced? Isn't this terrible job environment the same one I was in before? Didn't I move next door to the same kind of jerk?"

I'm talking about mistakes. Then you've got to close it off. In spite of the resistance you feel, you can do it. You can move; you can leave; you can do whatever you need to survive. It's as stupid as saying, "I'm now in quicksand. What should I do?" Somebody says, "I'm going to throw you a rope." You say, "No way. I'm going to stand here, and go under happily saying, 'See, this is my karma.'"

In *The Last Temptation of Christ,* Jesus said, "I had to do this." His time on Gethsemane was really something. He really *raged* against God. In one line that I love, he said, "I know God loves me. I wish He didn't."

And, of course, He does. In the knowledge of God's love, in the stretching of our soul to spiritual heights, it hurts. Anything hurts when it's coming alive. Have you ever watched a newborn baby? Whether it's animal or human, it stretches and moves, and you can see it strain for life. Or sit on your hand for a while, or have your leg in one place—what happens? When it begins coming back to life, how does it feel? Horrible, right? It tingles and burns. That's the way your soul is.

When the soul stretches, it *does* magnify the Lord, but we're so afraid to touch those edges of our own emotion. "What if I love too much and I'm hurt? What if I give it all and I'm disappointed?" And you will be. Yet what would it be like to have never given at all until you're empty? You'd never know that there's another living, breathing person, or even an ideal that you could empty it all out for. You know what we're so afraid of? If I empty it all out, will anything ever fill me up again? Oh, yes, to even greater depths.

Each time you empty yourself out in life, you get deeper. If you never do it, you stay very small and shallow. So give it all, and keep giving it all. You will still lose people in this life, but only on this Earth plane, and it's for a reason. Very few things are meant to be permanent on this plane. In giving up everything, there's a blessing from God. In giving it all up, something fills you up. That something, of course, is God.

However, do not choose to love people who are not worthy of your love. Now you say, "Well, how do I know that, Sylvia?" Because they're rotten. You can feel it because you're psychic enough. People can turn on you like bad meat. They go rancid, don't they? Then you should, for your own soul's sake, go on. Someone else will pick it up and make a stew out of it.

You can't be fiddling around with something that becomes stale to you. The staleness you perceive will become freshness to someone else. Think of the journey of your soul—you wend your way through life, experiencing, loving, caring, giving it all up. Think of yourself as a beacon of light. Go out and tell people your beliefs, how you feel about things. Get rid of your guilt and negativity.

Make your positive circle wider. Marry someone who is really different. You don't want all your kids to be the same. People think they should treat all their kids the same. I hope they don't, because they're all different. Perhaps at work, or even in your own family, you're treated poorly. People are mean to you. Don't let anybody treat you like that.

Don't you dare let anybody treat you as less than God, because you *are* God. You are a moving, breathing spark of God. Don't you dare allow yourself to be treated badly. Be good to yourself. Be kind. That's part of your karma.

Now, unfortunately, you have to expect that you will shock the person you've been carrying. That's your fault. You've done it— you've babied them. We do this, don't we? Then all of a sudden, we say, "Well, I don't choose to do that anymore," and they get mad at us. Then, we must stay strong and finish it. We must complete the circle, and that's hard. Do you know why? Because we're afraid that we won't be loved, aren't we?

And so, what does it matter? The greatest thing that I've learned is that it doesn't matter whether you love me. It *does* matter that I love you. Once I got that through my thick skull, it was wondrous. I just walk around with the joy of loving you. I don't expect you to love me back. That's wonderful—no more expectations of "payback." I've done that; haven't you? We start auditing in our mind, don't we? "I've done ten nice things for you today. Now I'm in the house cooking and cleaning and slaving. Do you say thank you? No." It doesn't matter. If I didn't want clean floors, then I wouldn't have wasted my time cleaning them. In the end, you do these things for yourself, no one else.

Misconceptions

Francine: I'd like to give you more information about what the "experiencing" part of karma really is. We know that there's such a thing as *retributive karma,* which is very rare. Many people will tell you that the reason your life is terrible is that you've done something bad in a past life. However, that's almost never the case, because you're experiencing for God.

When you experience heartaches in your daily life, please be fully assured that it's not because you've done some evil in a past life—unless, of course, you're a "dark" entity. Karma *does not* apply to dark entities, whose whole karmic experience is to disrupt, hurt, maim, and destroy. They can't maim you physically, but they maim your soul in the sense that you become despondent, with feelings of futility and despair.

This is why we have always been so adamantly against suicide, because such actions are caused by darkness, which has invaded your soul. It does not make you dark, but the "psychic attack" makes you *futile* enough so that you don't care to go on living anymore. *That* is what you should insulate yourself from.

Retributive karma is the least common aspect. It's very rare and only happens once in a great while. As Sylvia says, in her many years of counseling, she's found that she could count the retributive karma on one hand with fingers left over. That's absolutely a fact. Of all the thousands she's read for, she has rarely come across retributive karma—it's that rare. It's possible that, for example, a person had put somebody's eye out, and then that person would choose to come back in with one eye missing, but that would only be the *choice of experiencing* what they had done to another person—not out of retribution, but just to experience it.

Then you say, "Where is the justice for those being raped, hurt, and martyred?" It's hard for most people to believe or understand this, but every person *will pick* these experiences to fulfill their theme, or some other goal they have. You'll experience all aspects of life, either bad, good, horrific, or whatever. You'll have experiences in *everything*.

That doesn't mean that in some life you necessarily *have* to experience the Victimization theme. But *some* choose that to experience for God.

Sylvia will certainly agree that for every person who has lived through a horrendously difficult life, there are many hundreds who have had nonstressful lives, which you would think of as normal. They're not so dramatic—they may seem to be laborious, tiresome, boring lives—yet those people are also learning.

For one person, a trauma can be something very large. For another, that same trauma may seem quite minor. It depends on that person's individuality. When you rise above this life into the spiritual realm and realize when you look over this mass of humanity that's being sacrificed or hurt or starved (and it seems so unequal), in the long term, *it equals out.*

Everyone eventually gets to the Other Side, looks back, and most of the time says, "I did a good job. I experienced that." Only the *most advanced* souls pick horrifying experiences. Some do this because they want a brief life. Even though we look at the act as being hideous and heinous in many ways, realize it was that *soul choosing.*

Very often when you watch someone who skydives or does dangerous stunts, you wonder why. Well, they do it for the thrill. Karma is experiencing for your soul. You will pick innumerable experiences. Whether it's to get an illness, to be perfectly happy (which most entities are not capable of), or to have an infirmity of some type—all of those are experiences for Almighty God. So when you're going through your trials and tribulations, you must say to yourself, "Chalk another one up for *me*. I have *not* succumbed to grief, futility, or despair."

Above all this, there is a *joyous* part of life that says, "I *have* survived. I *have* jumped the hurdles. I *have* become magnificent in my experience for God" When you get into a really horrifying stage of grief, make sure that you put yourself above the body so that you're more or less flying above it.

Can "walk-ins" take over in hard times?

There is *no* such a thing as a "walk-in." I'm sure that every single one of you would have wished, at some point in life, to have somebody come in and finish a karmic experience. When you experience a lot of pain, grief, and despondency, wouldn't you just love to say, "Hey, somebody else take over"?

Too bad—you're in. You have to finish it. Nobody else can take over. It's a wonderful fantasy fairy-story, which possibly made other people feel good at a point in time. But it's *not* true.

However, there's a sense in which all your lives are equally real; that is in God's time. Each record is being viewed by God from every lifetime you've ever had. But you're in full consciousness experiencing right here and now. There's not some part of you on the Other Side observing, "I'm glad they are there and I am here." No. Only your guides say that.

There is, though, a phenomenon called the *karmic chain* that's quite similar; perhaps this is the root of the confusion. Sometimes, a person's karma becomes so strong that their karmic experience is passed to another entity to carry it on. So you're not only picking up your own experience, but you attached that unfinished job to your own chart. By doing that, you begin to live out the *unfinished* karma of someone else.

Let me give you an example. Sylvia's grandmother, Ada Coil, was a great psychic, very notable in Kansas City—so much so that there are still people to this day who pray to her. I'm sure that if she had been involved with full-blown Catholicism, she would have been sainted. When people pray to Ada, things get done because she was a magnificent entity. Her life span ended at 88.

Sylvia came along (not only by genetics) and asked to pick up that lineage. Of course, she was already going to be a psychic; that was all set. But she wanted to be even *more* so. So she picked up the threads of her grandmother. Later, Sylvia prayed and asked that one of her children, if it would create happiness, pick up the thread of *her* karma. Blessedly, Christopher picked up the thread and made it a cord. So the lineage goes on. This can happen with art, suffering, happiness, writing, or anything else.

You know how many times people say, "I'm living the same life that my mother or father did"? Psychology has all kinds of magnificent words for this such as *co-dependency* or *inherent traits*. They haven't yet gotten to the level of spirituality to realize that this soul has chosen to pick up the pieces.

Now, this can work in reverse, also. What you will do, many times, is either karmically continue that pain or suffering, or become the opposite. Don't you see how all of this begins to level out the apparent inequity?

Think of a large painting on a wall. Some people are working on the bottom part. Some are working on the top. All the artists together make one gigantic painting. They're all threading through to make something beautiful. Now, don't you see how you're also helping to put a paintbrush to the canvas? Your actions make a difference, no matter how trivial or boring they seem. Whenever the soul is directed toward a spiritual cause, that individual adds a little bit of color to the canvas and strengthens the picture.

Now, you also have a *collective group karma* that many people add to. That experience becomes beautiful. The more people that you involve in a group, the brighter that picture becomes. Each color then becomes richer. That's the whole purpose and reason for people congregating together as a church. It's not so much that God cares, but of course, it *magnifies God,* and thereby you magnify yourself.

However, group karma can also work in an adverse way such as in cults like the one led by Jim Jones. This is an example of karma gone awry. That experience was a *negative warp*. Yet, if you look at it in the broad scope, it made everyone aware of cultism. Sometimes there has to be a negative conglomerate, such as Dachau, as horrifying as that is, to make the world take notice.

Jim Jones, I will tell you without any doubt, was a dark entity. You cannot always judge that, but he definitely was. But those people that followed him were *not* dark. They were just susceptible to his persuasive misstatement of truth. Unfortunately, they went to the slaughter with him. Nevertheless, those souls still perfected. They went to the sacrificial altar to show other people. However, even when a warp develops like that, a *choice* still exists. That really was the option line for everyone in the group, and they just went awry on it. This is different than Dachau. Dachau was not an option; those people were driven to their deaths by brute force.

So, karmic chains are planned, not picked after birth?

It happens almost immediately *before* you come in. A life is planned intricately before the Council, your guides, and your master teachers. But there's always an optional chain that you can pull before you "drop through the hatch," as we say. It's like a last-minute term paper you can pick up for extra credit. Somebody could say, "I will write the book that my mother didn't finish." Or, "because so-and-so died early, I'll take it upon myself to make his works known."

So a person takes up the crucible, so to speak. An entity who has created a wrong usually tries to make it right in this life, and most of the time is successful. They might not make it up to the person they victimized, but they will create something good elsewhere to balance it out.

Can a nemesis follow us life after life?

Sometimes, for experiencing purposes. This individual can be the most hellish person in the world to you so that your soul can learn tolerance or patience. Sometimes those people are more powerful in their negativity than some good person who comes along. Then we all say, "But for the grace of God, there go I." How many times have you been influenced positively *because* you saw the evil in someone else that you never wanted to emulate. Those people, in a sense, are fulfilling (as insane as this is to say) their karmic roles better than these insipid types who profess goodness but never stand up for their beliefs.

That nemesis relationship is almost the opposite of being a kindred soul; they are the antithesis of your soul. They can follow you until you both just bang against each other hard enough that you learn. Such a soul can be gray or dark in many cases.

Do we learn from negative people?

Sure. If you don't meet anybody who rubs against you karmically, then you have nothing to learn from. Children are good for that. They exhibit negative behaviors but are not necessarily dark souls.

Sylvia said I was stuck in a "karmic dome" and to grab the golden thread to get out.

There is a strange phenomenon that happens occasionally. You can get caught by, and *domed in* by, someone else's karma. They begin to weave a web around you. At first you think you're running free, until you try to escape and find out you're trapped by the intricacies of their karma. Often this is done through financial disaster, deception, or even death. Some people never break free from that dome. They say, "Well, I'm caught. Rather than struggle, I'm just going to sit in here and whine about it."

The golden thread is your spirituality. It draws you out. You reach for God's hand, make a break for it, and crash through. It's like thinking that the spider web is solid. Then you hit against it, and you find that it gives. Some people don't have sense enough to break it. They don't go to the edge of it.

Weren't you ever caught up in your parents' illusory webs? They say, "If you do that, something terrible will happen." You're convinced that this is true. Many times it's a self-fulfilling prophecy, though, since you believe it so thoroughly.

When did God write the main chart?

He wrote the charts from the very "beginning," and He continues to have them written, so to speak—they include the global patterns we must struggle with. All of that was written on the larger scale as a stage for our individual evolvement.

But, you say, "What about the homeless, the people who are starving, and the wars?"

You must go back to the original premise: *Those people wrote it* in their chart. Now, are you under any obligation to pray and help? Of course you are. That's how, as we go along, we *enhance* our chart. The chart as originally written is very simplistic, but we gather extra credit along the way.

Certainly you're supposed to travel to and from work, but why not stop along the way, pick some roses, and help somebody out of a ditch? You're not "off track" by doing that. That's what life is about—to give of ourselves. Too often, you see somebody in a fast car just flying down the highway without a care for anybody else—and then somebody else in an old jalopy stops and helps everyone.

Does guilt affect us in planning a life?

Most entities are *not born* with guilt, but everything in your society programs it. Baptism was originally meant to get rid of any past life carryovers and to cleanse you of karmic debt and guilt. The minute the soul hits the human body, it automatically assumes guilt for some reason. We don't know why that is. It's almost like, if you put a boat in the water long enough, it will form barnacles. It just seems to come with the flesh. It is a stamp, a stigma to the soul.

Even if you're not raised in a religious environment, your parents give it to you in human life: "You hurt your mother; you did this or that. You are bad; you're going to hell. God does not love you."

On and on it goes, so the soul is stamped again with guilt. That's why those born in primitive cultures are better to each other than "civilized" people. Educated people will create war more often. Now, primitive people will fight if there's been an invasion of territory or because of food—but not just because they are mad or have *avarice*. They don't make war on another human being unless provoked, just as animals do not.

But the more educated and sophisticated people are, the more they think, and the more they become complex. They develop an awareness of avarice and greed, then *they create these acts*. They are told they should not; then, of course, *they have guilt*. It becomes a vicious cycle. Guilt is a real, functional emotion, but it was never meant to get out of hand. In other words, if you do something with *malice of intention*, you *should* have guilt. But most people do not. Most people do things inadvertently, and then turn around and go, "Oh my God." In retrospect, they assume guilt needlessly.

Can we disrupt karma by saving a drowning baby?

There are cultures who absolutely believe that if a baby falls in the water, they should just watch the baby sink all the way to the bottom. That's what we call the *noninterfering* interpretation of karma, which is just as vile as *too much* interference. They don't have sense enough to realize that they've been given the *sense* to pull the baby out. It's ridiculous to let a child die because of such a belief.

Dharma

Let's speak briefly about dharma—a very interesting phenomenon that links with the karmic chain. Dharma is the responsibility that you assume along the journey of life.

You can pick the flowers, help the homeless, and do all those things you want to do. You can accept or reject responsibilities as you wish.

When you come in, you don't pick all your dharma. Let's say that you came in with the theme of Experiencer or Catalyst. The more activated themes tend to form a protective circle. They'll pick up other people's problems more so than the average person. The more spiritual you become, sometimes, the more dharma you will incur.

Dharma is only another word for *responsibilities*. But be careful of that, because spirituality and the magnification of the soul also carry with them warnings. Be very careful that you do *not* pick up somebody else's karma while they are living. You do not want to get caught in that.

So when you're picking up these responsibilities—taking care of others and doing good—start asking yourself, "How much does it bother me? How much fun am I having? How much do I enjoy it? How much is it thwarting me? How much do I resent it?" When you come upon these phrases, then you can rest assured that you have picked up *too much* dharma.

You can simply be aggravated and tired, but if in your heart you truthfully feel that you could never do anything different, then you're not *that* tired. But when you get to the point that a spouse or child or a person or a job has now become more of a horrendous responsibility than a joy, you're off your path. You're not running on the blue line. It's a very spiritual issue to ask what's good for you. That's not being selfish. Ask yourself, "What am I getting out of it?" If you keep coming up with big zeros, don't do it anymore.

A spiritual theme means that you will search for spirituality in everything you do. The marvelous by-product of this spiritual knowledge is that when you're confronted with problems, you can say, "Even though it seems crazy, I'm going to use the silver and white lights. I'm going to use mirrors and encase myself in gold."

Pretty soon, even though you might not expect it, positive things begin to happen. You call on Mother God to wield her sword and cult through negativity. This doesn't mean that Mother God in Her glory comes down and cuts off somebody's head in front of you. No. It means that the threads of these dharmic connections can be severed.

Sometimes you need outside help. Certain bright, shining humans will come in and crack the dome of despair. Such people have taken on a dharma, a responsibility, to crack the darkness. Now, what is aggravating to you and to me and to all of us is, how many times do some people need to be saved? I'm sure you have friends like this, about whom you say, "I have repeatedly taken them out of darkness, but when I'm not around, they crawl right back into it again."

Leave them there. Let someone else continue this particular quest, because you're not able to help them anymore. You need to shine brighter, to help other people who can be helped. That's one of the hardest things to know: when it's time to move on.

Are we sometimes tested in life?

Everyone has periods of their lives that are charted as tests. It's written in to have those tests, and the details are blocked from your guides, because if you had any reciprocation or help, there would be no test. This is why Sylvia, or any psychic, knows nothing about their own life.

If they did, then they would win the lottery and have an ideal life with great marriages, wonderful children, and everything perfect. Even I, being Sylvia's guide, am learning all the time, the same as your guide is. So the blockages are written in, too. It's very much like getting lost in the woods with your radio dead. Those "desert" periods are all purposely there.

If you always have someone telling you, "Go this way, go that way," your life would be perfect. You would just skip down the highway while everybody else was crashing. But the guide is learning along with the person they're guiding.

Certainly we guides have higher knowledge. But if we were perfect, we would not be guides. Both the guides and those in life are perfecting.

Do some of us have more than one spirit guide?

You need more. Sylvia has four—you just don't hear much about the other ones that she has. She has Axier, Raheim, Solomon, and myself.

Is it true that sometimes people cling to life and refuse to cross over?

Yes, they can just linger and linger. It's a good idea to try to talk them over. Say, "*Go.* You've worn out your welcome. The only thing you're accomplishing is aggravation." That's *not* mean to say. Put it on yourself. Say to them, "For my sake, for your loved ones, let's end it now." However, this does *not* mean euthanasia. Simply give them permission to go.

Have you ever had guests who just stood at the door and kept talking, until you were ready to kick them into their car, and say, "Leave"? They just wear you out talking and staying.

Do guides go through pain with us?

We suffer along with the person terribly. For therapy, we go to the Council. Occasionally they yell at us, but more often I yell at them, screaming that it was not supposed to go this way. Yes, I've even gone over their heads, as all guides will. The Council is very much like the Greek Senate. We can appeal to a higher power and get something done, not like your so-called democracy.

We will have a period of counsel, then we can consult with those who have gone behind the Godhead. If that doesn't work, we can go directly to Azna (Mother God). We can have an audience. I also have to realize that the time span is different. All guides have to become humanized enough to feel. If a guide is too elevated or too unfeeling, they don't care.

"Humanized" guides are kept separate on the Other Side. You know it is certain that you have all been, or will be, a spirit guide to another at some time. When you're a guide, you move yourself down a little bit lower in your spirituality. It doesn't mean that the rest of the entities ignore you, but you're so involved in guiding the person and learning along with them that you don't get to really mix with the upper echelon, so to speak. When the lifetime of your person is over, then you ascend, also. It's very much like what the guide Fletcher said after Arthur Ford died. Fletcher was asked through another medium if he would ever choose to be a guide again. He said, "Not by any stretch of the imagination."

I'm sure that all guides feel the same way. So, most likely, you will want to do it only once.

Can we ask for lessons to speed up?

Yes, to be sped up, and even dropped. We can also petition that the process be sped up for the other people involved. We don't feel the negativity, but we can see it coming. Ask for that to dissipate.

Guides can open up windows of opportunity that you really should complete for your own dharma. If you let those windows pass, you'll say, "I had the key. I should have jumped in, but I walked right past." In this case, do not despair; you lost a little bit of ground, so to speak, but then another door will open.

Through human endeavor, prayers can be answered. We always think that it's God Who must answer prayers, but so many times you'll hear, "*You* are the answer to my prayers." That other person is God's hand moving. His help will usually come through a human form.

It would be wonderful if we could all pray, "Let us have money," and a giant basket of cash would fall. And, certainly, God in His omnipotent grace could make money appear in this fashion. But you see, what you miss is that some people are karmically supposed to give and help whenever possible.

Do you have spiritual celebrations on the Other Side?

Yes. We also celebrate Azna. We constructed an absolutely beautiful temple of glistening gold, silver, and glass for the night of your summer solstice. We had millions and millions of candles, and there were countless millions of us coming down golden steps.

Each time we have one of these festivals, we build a different temple. Sometimes we have it spiraled, sometimes domed, sometimes crystal. Azna just walks down. It's all on the scanner, so you can see the festivals if you wish when you come Home to the Other Side.

What was your life like, Francine?

I lived from A.D. 1500 to 1519. I had a daughter. I died because I took a spear in the chest to protect her, and that was that. But during those 19 years—you may not have known this—I was a High Priestess in the *Aztec-Incan* community, in which we worshiped the Mother Goddess.

Becoming More Spiritual

Along with our discussion about karma and dharma, I would like to add a smattering about how you can become more spiritual. Everyone is asking about this now. Not to be negative, but the world turns in a manner that's strange and ferociously different from what you would ever know it to be. Your news constantly shows the terror in your streets and the world—someone always starts quoting Revelations to you, speaking of the end of the world. I'm sorry to say it's *not true*. It would be so much easier if there was an ending to all this so that you could all come Home, but unfortunately, there's a long time to go until the end. With that in mind, please keep a positive attitude. Probably never before in the history of this planet has there been a better time than now to grow, perfect your soul, and become more advanced in the mind and eye of God.

It's almost like this planet has turned into a very elite universe of its own. It has become a university to which only the strongest will be admitted—that sounds very elitist, but some people are not seeking after knowledge, and instead are blindly following the word of one or two sources. They will never find their inner core of knowledge as you will, because you seek and search.

The one thing that you must guard against is ego. We have watched this very carefully and have seen an increasing number of ego structures beginning to rise up. This you must guard against. The ego is probably your worst enemy.

If there is any such thing as satanism (if you even use that silly word), it is your own ego being impressed with yourself. No matter what job you do, you must keep in mind that someone can come after you and do that job, too. This is not self-deprecating—it is true. Even though you may glory in your own soul and your own uniqueness, watch the words that come out of your mouth. Your words can be so hateful, so authoritative. That's the only way that you move yourself back, as it were, and take yourself *out* of a spiritual life.

Say instead, "I will not be involved with my own false ego, but my true 'I Am.'" The latter is the sum total of what you are, beautiful and unique. When you start thinking that you are "so important," that's where you fall prey to darkness.

As far as I can remember in my lifetime (even though it was short), the minute I felt that I was of some great importance, I was always knocked down a peg or two by something that came soon after that. So whenever you get too impressed with yourself, something always hammers on your kneecap.

The karma that ensues from that is almost instantaneous. This "instant karma" ensures that the minute you feel irreplaceable, then someone will prove how really mistaken you are. It almost seems that you are sending out the message: "No one can ever do this job as well as I can." Then, sure enough, someone comes up and does it better.

So karmic retribution is aimed at false ego?

It is never directed against the true "I Am." Here on the Other Side, we have true ego. The false one only occurs in the human vehicle. This can happen anywhere in life. You say, "My car is shinier than your car," and then you get a dent in it. "My legs are better than yours," and you fall down and break one. "My hair is better than his," and then you lose it.

It seems to be a direct assault against yourself. Now, you've written this into your chart. We have not. You've written in marvelous ego busters that come into play anytime you're getting too impressed with yourself.

Get *out of* yourself, not into yourself. Larry [Sylvia's husband] has an expression that I love: "Some people's world goes as far as their eyelashes." When your world centers completely around *yourself,* you're stepping onto dangerous ground. This is true whether you're focused on how great you are *or* what is wrong with you and how lowly you are. It is still I, I, I. When a person is constantly morbid, cranky, and ill-tempered, that affects their aura; it goes out to others, is reflected back, and returns to slap you.

"Poor me. Why don't I have enough? Why am I in this mess? I deserve better. Why am I always the one that is picked on?" That is a dangerous mind-set, only because you start building dark cinder blocks around yourself. I use cinder blocks as an analogy because they're easier to cut through. Dark entities build granite blocks, and they stay within them. You just build up cinder blocks. That's why I think you've always used the expression, "I am blocked." You *are* blocked, but only by your own false ego.

Take life with a sense of humor. This is always the best way to dispel karma. A sense of humor seems to be taken so lightly, but it's probably one of the *truest* ways that God's love is shown. Did you realize that? Laughter brings about happiness, which dispels darkness.

If a person can make you laugh, that brings about joy. It fills your soul. A person without a sense of humor becomes darker and darker and darker. If you can laugh at yourself, it's the best. You're now advancing to a different level. If you can laugh at yourself and the vehicle that you're in (whether you're heavy, thin, headachey, or tired), then the pain of life all slips away. It really, really will not matter.

Most of you were fortunate enough to be born with a functional "I Am." That is very important. The false ego only comes about in life. Remember, your problems are only important because you've affirmed them to be so. You've always heard, "If I can't make myself happy, I can't make anyone else happy." No. That's wrong. When you make others happy, that's when you make yourself happy. That is the law of the universe.

People say, "But I can't find a way to make myself happy." That's because you're sitting in a room all the time trying to cheer yourself up. The only way to do it is to focus outward to other human beings, to make *them* happy. In that, light shines back on you. You were never meant to be an isolated entity, hiding your light, never making anybody laugh or smile. It seems that with so many of you, if you smiled, your face would crack off.

People will invariably say, "I have nothing to smile about." In truth, you have *everything* to smile about:

- God loves you.
- Your soul is perfecting.
- You have the courage to be here.
- You are a spiritual warrior for God.

That is something to smile about. There are so many people who take their outward appearance as being all-important. But, as Sylvia has said for many years, "With some of the most physically beautiful people in the world, the more you get to know them, the *uglier* they become. Or conversely, when one seems to be very homely, as you get to know them, their beauty *shines*."

Have you ever noticed that with loved ones, the more you get to know them, the less you even notice their features? What matters most is the presence of the person. Their *essence* is where true beauty resides, not the body.

Now, I could go on and on about retributive karma resulting from malicious intent. I'll tell you how it operates: Malicious intent means that you've actively begun a process leading to the harm of another person. Don't worry about the vengeful thoughts that come across your mind when someone has hurt you. There's no power associated with your mind's fantasy trips about revenge; just don't act on these feelings.

Don't always be so concerned with how your words fall, especially if you don't mean them to hurt. If they're received in a bad way, that's the listener's fault. For example, say that someone has been terribly hurt, and you, in defense, go after that wrongdoer in order to make things right. That's not retributive.

Let's say you can't defend yourself, and someone comes forward and defends you. That's a good thing. There's no malicious intent. You're using righteous anger on the offending person. More than anything, defend the dignity of your soul or your loved ones.

Do not let people walk all over you—say or do something! Jesus was the one who went to the money changers and turned over their tables. He was not meek, mild, or timid. He went after injustices with conviction and strength.

When should we stop giving to others?

When it impedes the perfection of your soul. The challenge is to discern who can be helped from those who simply want to use you. Do not waste your time on one person who doesn't want to get better, when there are ten others you could be helping who *will* get better. If you always carry someone, then their legs won't work. Ask God to help you know who is worthy of your time.

What if we use profanity?

No words are offensive to God. If they were, then God would be humanized. He *cannot* get upset about any word you could say. God is far beyond monitoring your vocabulary. Can you imagine God evaluating every single, solitary word that you utter? If you refer to fecal matter, how could He possibly care? God made your body with fecal matter. Fornication words have *no* bearing on God—He made people to couple.

Why would God care if you use "profanity"? That was all started by religious leaders in order to keep people under their control, just the same as dress codes, behavior rules, or anything else. Be reasonable. God is constantly in the state of loving. He has no emotions regarding all that silly stuff. I know it's very hard for you to remember that God is above human concerns. But you must, if you are to understand the true God.

Certainly some modes of expression can be offensive to you. You don't want people going around just spewing profanity all over the place, because it's offensive. The God *within you* might react, and that is valid. But profanity does not denigrate the soul or affect God..

There has been profanity all down through history. It just depends on the customs of the area. You can go to other countries and say the simplest of words, and they could be interpreted negatively. So you see, like morality and spirituality, profanity is situational. In Kenya, women can be in public bare-breasted, but in the U.S., it's illegal.

All of these issues fall away when you realize that you do not *want* to be offensive to the other gods around you. Everyone is part of God. So if you need to verbally emote, go in the bathroom and "cuss a blue streak," as they say. It doesn't matter. God isn't going to listen in and condemn you. Your hell is already here. As Milton said, "The mind is its own place, and it can make a heaven of hell, or a hell of heaven."

What happens to one's karma in crimes of passion or insanity?

There is karma attached, but it's so minimal. For example, if a mother sees her child attacked and she reacts by shooting the attacker, then there's no karma. That's passion. Similarly, if she were insane or driven to that point, very little karma is attached to that. *Everything is intention.* A pure motive carries no karma.

It can be difficult to determine whether harmful intent was there or not. So many times, after the deed is done, you start questioning yourself about what your intentions were. Then you build up unnecessary guilt for yourself, instead of just giving it to God. Now, this doesn't allow you to go out and do anything you want. Intention is so vitally important. When you really get into the spiritual throes of this theology, you will question your intent. How important is it to seek revenge? How important is it to inflict hurt? What are you really accomplishing? Are you doing this for your own ego, or are you trying to right something?

At the last minute, mercy can take over, and that's even better. That reflects a more highly evolved soul. Mercy is the release of hate. You get right down to the point where you want to annihilate someone, and then you give it to God.

Oriental philosophy says, "When you seek revenge, you must dig two graves." It's better to look at the other's truth. Realize where they are coming from, and even where you are coming from. Spirituality means enlightenment. When you live more fully within your spirituality, you will see motives. They will be made clear to you by the Holy Spirit. You will see where people are coming from.

Do you see malicious intent on your side?

Oh, yes, absolutely we do. It really puts a mark on your chart. You've already requested that you get what we call "the red slash." When you come back, you're not judged, but you see what red marks are in your record. Then you sit for a long time in the Hall of Wisdom and talk to the Council. You're actually *counseled* on that.

What about curses or voodoo?

When someone sends you negative energy, they might not even be aware of it, but you can feel their jealousy, avarice, or envy. This is called a *psychic attack*. It usually bounces directly back to the sender, although sometimes it takes a little bit longer. Sylvia feels that these so-called voodoo curses, or candle-lighting ceremonies for a fee, are so ridiculous. What happens is that those people simply heap darkness upon themselves, but it has no impact on you.

Usually, you don't see these people getting any retributive karma back. You may wonder how this can be—the reason is that they're dark. So you ask, "Why don't these evil people 'get it' in life?" They never will. However, they will never go to the Other Side, either; they keep coming back into life. Earth is the only reality they have. The retribution they suffer is that they *never* go to the Other Side. *That's enough!* They never see God; they just keep recycling.

Would it help if you enacted retribution on them? No. It does not affect them; it would only affect white entities. Dark entities are never hurt.

So how do you stop "darks" from impinging upon you? Neutralize them by sending white light. Think of yourself encased in lead. Think of them sending you arrows, which bend and fall to the ground. Surround them with lead and a circle of mirrors facing inward to them. It really works.

Do we take karma to the Other Side?

No, all you do is look at your "score sheet." Most of you will be very surprised when there are *not* a lot of red slashes. Too many people walk around feeling that they are "sin-filled" and vile before God, but that is not true at all. If there is any sin at all, it is the sin of despair.

One thing you have to watch out for is the warping of your ego structure. Everyone comes in with a need to be loved, because the human body makes you separate from each other; it makes you terribly alienated. You feel so isolated that you may go off-track until your intellect regains control.

To gain acceptance, sometimes you get involved in living someone else's karmic experience. You may find yourself living their life, and I don't mean out of joy. That's deadly to your perfection. Your soul will not be injured, but it can negate your chart.

Should you find yourself in a karmic dome, then look at your intentions. If they're pure, you may not like what you're doing, but ultimately you're doing it for God. That's a valid path. But if you're simply indulging your ego, then you should get out of it.

There's no way in this world that God doesn't want everyone to be happy. That's one thing you can be sure of. The only pure emotions are love and happiness—those are sisters of each other.

You can just do so much, and then you've got to get away from it. Some people, tragically, want to be maintained through their whole life. They need endless counseling. I've found so many people symbiotically hanging on to another, feeling important because they give constant counsel. No one needs that. It's deadly for both of you. After you've counseled and helped, you can't keep sacrificing your life.

Some people are tremendously thrilled with taking care of an invalid or a sick person or somebody that is maudlin or depressed. You say, "How do they do it?" They're happy doing it. But if you're not happy doing it, you're wrecking the light that you have.

The exception is with small children who still need your care. Any parent has taken on an added burden of responsibility. Childbearing is dharma—it's a *responsibility*. You have the child; therefore, you're responsible for him or her.

Sometimes you'll find someone in need and you were meant to help them. Now, do you take them into your home forever? No. Do not take this to extremes. But if you love doing something (we go back to intent), keep doing it. If you love taking many children with disabilities into your home, then God bless you for that. But *don't* look at someone else and say, "You're inferior to me because you haven't done this."

That's where the false ego comes in. People start making a list in their own mind about how good they've been—or how bad. You must realize that you preplanned to have karmic lessons, including overcoming your false ego, and being kind. So watch your words that have unkind motives. Get outside of yourself. That's a responsibility you all have.

Now, perhaps you have a mother who is vicious, cruel, mean, and hateful. Are you supposed to stay and take her abuse? No. The same goes for an employer or spouse. You need not keep approaching that person to constantly be hit sideways and demeaned. Doing that will stifle your spirituality and put out your inner light. Then you're truly off-track.

Now, you still need to avoid being mean and intentionally hurting them. Neutralize the situation, do what you must for them, and then move away. It won't prey on your mind if you don't *allow* it to. Realize that this person is simply an obstacle placed here for your development of tolerance. As you become more spiritual, people whom you love, who share similar spirituality, will be far closer to you than any blood.

Spirituality exacts a tremendous price. When you begin to change spiritually and no longer allow people to walk over you, some won't like the changes in you. Family is the first place in which this will rise. Then you have to find people who are spiritual enough to walk the same path with you.

Can there be dharmic consequences?

If you're a woman driving down a lonely road and you see a car stopped on the side of the road, would you be smart to stop? Of course not. That would be stupid, because the potential for harm is too great. So, here we have the primary obligation, which must be to fulfill your own chart.

You ask, "Shouldn't I just rush into every battle?" No. That is stupidity. You must realize that the soul and the body you are saving could be your own. You have a right to take precautions with the body that you're using. The vehicle you chose has been lent to you by God. You do not have the right to abuse it.

How do we protect ourselves from those who don't understand our spirituality?

First of all—and this is the hardest part—by trying to be kind and sympathetic with them. Sometimes this makes them more furious, but your spiritual progress will become so tremendous that a lot of people will not know you. That's all right. You do *not* want to carry those people with you through all eternity anyway.

You just need to "white light" them and send God's grace around them. In many ways, it sounds very passive, but it's really *very active and dynamic*. It coincides with concepts in ancient Eastern religions as well.

Chapter Three

LIFE THEMES

Francine: I want to talk to you about your *essence*, which is that spark of God that you're made of, which will continue with you through all eternity. This part of God was individually created in you, uniquely shaped and formed, and sent on its way to return with its individuality back to God. You will never lose this identity; it is the very core of your being.

I'm making a point of this because in so many religions, it's purported that when you reach a level of perfection, you go into some nebulous mass and get lost in a sea of anonymity. You don't. That is never possible. In absorbing and companionably taking on this individual essence of God, you elevate to a point of Godliness, with a distinct persona.

Most people are afraid to say out loud that they are God. But they *are*. This has nothing to do with ego. It has to do with the Divine spark housed in your soul. Your divinity cannot be smothered, regardless of what behavioral overlays you may acquire. Cross, cranky, infirm, ill, mean at times, not feeling good—these emotions have nothing to do with your individual essence. They only have to do with behavior that's acquired from living in your world.

Let me tell you the different ways in which your perfection is brought about, because knowledge brings freedom. Your spark rolls through these experiences, gathering as it goes. The only problem is that in human form, you don't know how to get rid of all the dirt that collects in between the sparkles.

That's my job—to tell you how to clean out the dirt caked on your star. It has been acquired from many areas. Most of the negativity you have absorbed is not from time or space or location. It always comes from other entities. Animals and places don't create it.

"But," you may say, "there are places I can't stand." That's because of the negativity that has been put there by people—for example, perhaps people have been murdered or hurt there. Even a swamp might not be bad, except for the treachery of stepping in the wrong place. What you do is gather some of the essence of that.

It's marvelous to say to yourself every day, "I want my essence cleaned." It's as simple as housecleaning. Rinse clean of the day's negativity. I know that some of you use the white light and mirrors, but actually think of your soul as a sparkler that needs to be shined and freed of the mud of life.

Most of the time, you don't even realize that you're picking up the dirt of life, such as moods, negativity, heartaches, or pain. The problem is that the more your spiritual channel is open, the more apt you are to get some dirt in with the clear water. Think of water running clean and pure into your soul. You can never overdo this, or be too scrupulous, even if you did it every hour. I do it right before bed to help with nightmares or restlessness.

Take grief, for instance. One may come over to the Other Side to visit loved ones many times. That's not bad, but when somebody departs, you're apt to visit too much and return more drained than before. White visiting, your mind is not resting. That's why you wake up feeling that you have been with them but they're not there, and they ought to be—why aren't they? You've been visiting them. That's not wrong, but say to yourself, "I want to stay in," at least for the next couple weeks so that you're not so tired. That will help reduce the feeling that if you turn around, they'll be there.

How do we achieve this rinsing effect?

Envision yourself standing in a beautiful waterfall with the sun shining on you; see the water peeling away the dead layer of skin, and you stand there bright and shiny with baptismal water running over you. As the water hits you, you turn more and more golden.

You can have the water start out azure blue at the top, then turn from to green to purple to gold. Make sure the gold hits you under the waterfall. You feel that your soul is being refreshed. You'll truly be given the grace of the Holy Spirit.

This is wonderful to use. It's something that is tangible to the earth, because there again you're paying homage to Azna. Water is of the Mother—healing, purifying, and baptismal. So every day you rinse away your cares. That's why no matter how tired you are, if you bathe or shower, you'll be rejuvenated. You've taken off the outer coating of negativity. After you shower, always towel off using upward motions. This is invigorating and renewing.

It's unfortunate that such rituals are no longer as common as they were in ancient times. The dove has long symbolized the purity of a soul rinsed clean of all the tragedies of life. The early Gnostics did this intermittently with each other—not only symbolically and meditatively, but also in reality. The baptismal ritual was originally no more than a spirit-healing process. You know this is true. Consider all the rituals based upon bathing and rinsing, both in hot and cool water.

You've all heard the expression, "Time heals all wounds." If you engage in rituals, then time speeds up, and healing becomes quicker. When your pain softens and becomes manageable, we see it because your aura begins to turn bluish, or sometimes yellow. When we see you in anger or terrible grief, the color becomes flame red. In terrible depression, we see it become very muddy brown and sometimes black. That has nothing to do with you being a white or dark entity. It's your aura, a manifestation that we see.

Remember, also, that we can't read your mind unless you allow us to. If you were to ask me, I couldn't read your mind unless you granted me permission. So we must look at your aura to discern your emotional state. We don't take away the experience; we just help take the sharp edges off.

In your learning process, you can also perfect *without* the jagged edges. You experience not only through your own life, but through people you love. You know this is true. When someone you love is being hurt or persecuted, you have empathy, pain, and a feeling of despondency on behalf of that person.

Raheim: One way to grow spiritually is through sharing. If you can listen to a story and empathize or sympathize with another person about what they've gone through, you don't have to experience it. That doesn't mean that I want you to run out and hear all the awful stories that you possibly can so that you feel you've experienced it, but the word *vicarious* takes on deeper meaning here.

Haven't you ever had someone tell you a story, and the pathos was so great that you actually felt you'd gone through it with them? In doing so, you don't have to experience it again. Think about that. Time after time, you've experienced certain patterns in a million, myriad ways. You don't have to experience them again unless you haven't learned them yet. In that case, you keep picking up the same pattern until it's finished.

Francine: No one is strong enough to rule out our past-life memories. You come into every life with them. They're part of you.

Carrying this further, on the Other Side, you may merge with a person and experience what they did in a lifetime. In this way, you're perfecting by absorbing their experience. When you do this, you don't have to go through what they did. Actually, you're only getting the information content, not the full emotionality.

Many people can empathize with what it might feel like to lose a child. Touching that grief, they say, "I've gotten close enough; I don't want to touch it all the way." But on the Other Side, we are insulated by love, comfort, and security. There are no financial worries or cares, no fear of illness or any of those other things. We can share the knowledge of that type of pain without *having* the same pain. Life is so hard for you. You live in a world isolated by walls. I find it so depressing to come into Sylvia's body, because it's so confining. But it's most wondrous to speak to you.

Of course, I have a body on my side, but it's highly mutable, and I can merge with other entities who have come over. I can share their experiences.

Is it good or bad to be an organ donor?

It's fine to do that. We don't need our organs when we come over anyway. It is written in the Bible: "Greater love hath no man than to give up his life [or parts of the body] for another."

How much pain is shared in merging?

It's like watching yourself go through surgery and feeling bad about it, but not needing any anesthetic. The merging imparts not so much the emotional, as the intellectual, knowledge of what a person went through, which is much less shocking to the soul. But at least you're assimilating some of it. If we were to experience the total emotion, it would be a horrible thing for us. Then my side would not be a joyous place. The only emotions that we really experience to the utmost are the positive emanations such as love, happiness, joy, peace, and so on.

You go to Earth not for intellectual knowledge, but for emotional knowledge. We are the experiencing, emotional side of God.

I want you to notice that in severe grief or abandonment, if you've ever cried truly hard, there's a funny kind of a wail that audibly comes up out of the soul. The ancients knew this and called it the wailing, the keening, or the cry. Most primitive women and men let out these high-pitched wails or cries in extreme grief. In the British Isles, this keening brings up the "banshee," which is a construction of this cry that actually condenses itself into a form, and is heard and felt by the subconscious.

When your soul is in pain, allow yourself, meditatively, to go to a field and keen. Let yourself scream out this primitive cry, this wail that wants to emanate from your lips. Notice how similar the cry is to that of a baby's. Notice that when young children cry like this, we know they're all right. Why? The first sound you hear is that piercing shriek. Most of that has to do with the fact that they're furious about being down here again; they remember how bad it was to be here and how heavy the body was. The soul sets up the cry.

The immature emotional self within you can only grow through letting the tears come forward and letting the child grow. You've been taught religiously and culturally, through eons of time, that you're not supposed to release that emotional side of yourself. But this is like keeping a child cooped up in a very small pen. That's what you've done to the emotional side of yourself. The little person inside you never grows any bigger.

Men, unfortunately, have a worse time. Even more than women, they're told not to cry or show emotion. What happens, then? They become repressed in this, and eventually they die earlier. Women who keep their emotions submerged also get very cantankerous, embittered, lonely, and isolated. Why? They're not allowed to stretch that emotional side within them and grow.

Your world touts intellectual achievement as being the ultimate, doesn't it? How much schooling have you had? What is your education? How well do you speak? How much have you read? All that is fine, but it's not nearly as important as the emotional side.

People who live by their emotionality are fulfilling their destiny more so than the so-called intellectuals. This is not to put down intellectual pursuit, but both sides must rise. On the Other Side, we already have the intellectual knowledge, so your plane is for stretching emotionally. Yet when you got down here, you were told, "Don't cry. Don't let your inner child come out."

How many of you express your loving side, even to the point of going somewhere with friends, getting an ice-cream cone, or going for a ride? That is the child. Have a party. Play dress-up. Admit to yourself that you're a child inside—that you still hurt and still get lonely. If people talk badly about you, you get upset. I don't mean being a petulant fit-thrower—that's something else entirely.

Don't let people tell you to "grow up." That has no connection to what is real.

Theme vs. Karma

By now you know that karma refers to experiences for the soul and the lessons you must learn. Your karma started at the very second that your spark emanated from the Divine Sparkler, by which Sylvia and I always mean the "Godhead." As it traveled through time—regardless of how long you took to come in or how many lives you've chosen to experience—you're still going to fulfill at least two life themes.

Themes are frames of mind. They are situations you must push against to learn through. Since you must learn through them, they won't be easy. You will find, most of the time, that you pick up a primary and secondary theme. Themes can overlap. In other words, if you're a Cause Fighter, you might be a Builder, also. Not only do you serve the cause, but you also help build one.

Also, you will see that there are different stages of progression. I know that in life, you often feel that you're inching along or aren't really on track. Whenever you have these worries, it's a sign that you *are* on the right track. A derailed person *never* seeks truth, never questions, never searches for spirituality, and never searches for their inner self.

Before you came into life, you may have viewed every single path once—every nuance, shortcut, and detour—to find out what would best aid the major theme. That's why, when you start veering off too far, you become depressed. The soul tries to remind you through depression that you're off-track; illness may occur if you get too far off.

Everyone has their own path to take, so don't pattern yourself after someone else. You may have hero-worship or love or respect for another, but your path is your own. People often ask, "Am I on the right path?" You began the journey on the right path. Such questions about your true identity are, in themselves, a continuous spiritual journey. If you think that everyone feels this way, turn to a casual acquaintance and ask, "How's your spirituality these days?" Most people will give you a blank stare.

That certainly doesn't mean that you should develop an ostentatious spirituality, in which you focus on being more evolved than others. But there's a type of separation that happens when you become more spiritually evolved. In finding this marvelous, euphoric spirituality, the only people that you want to be close to are those *on the same path*.

45 Life Themes

Sylvia: From thousands of hypnotic sessions, here are the Life Themes I've discovered so far:

Activator—The focus here is to perform tasks that others have failed to accomplish. These may be truly gargantuan or quite menial, but the focus is always on getting the job done right. Activators, often called activists, are the turnaround artists or the trouble-shooters of the world, the ones who successfully reverse failure. Naturally, these entities are in great demand and so have a tendency to spread themselves too thin. Activators should make every effort to confine their energies to tasks where a genuine opportunity to achieve beneficial change exists.

Aesthetic Pursuits—Music, drama, painting, sculpting, and writing are included in this category. An aesthetic theme is not to be confused with a little "flair" for one of those enterprises. When an aesthetic theme is present, the entity is driven by his or her innate talent. A need to create manifests itself at a young age and dominates the individual's entire life. If the secondary theme is a complementary one, the entity has a long and productive career. If not, any acclaim and privilege the entity receives may lead to tragedy. The agonized existence of Vincent van Gogh reflects a tragic case of a conflicting secondary theme.

Analyzer—Not only does this entity want to know everything, but how it works and why. Analyzers are afraid they will miss something or that some detail will be overlooked. The rest of us learn from their continuing scrutiny of the most minute detail. These entities thrive in scientific or highly technical settings, where their skills are vital. In everyday life situations, their challenge is to let go and trust the senses. Analyzers should, after a discreet analysis of the behavior of others, ask the Holy Spirit for enlightenment to transcend the physical evidence.

Banner Carrier—The first lieutenant of the Cause Fighter (defined later) may be found picketing, demonstrating, or possibly lobbying; these entities also fight the battle against injustice. The key to success in perfecting this theme is moderation, tact, and discrimination. It is far better for these entities to select one cause and see it through than to scatter their impact among many.

Builder—These entities are the cornerstones of society, the unsung heroes and heroines of wars, home life, and organizations. Good parents are often builders, enabling their children to go on to a much larger canvas. Without these cogs, the wheels would never turn, yet builders rarely receive credit for the accomplishments made possible by their efforts. They need to keep in mind that not all prizes are won on this plane of existence. Often those who get the credit on Earth are not perfecting as rapidly as the builders who help to make their accomplishments possible.

Catalyst—Here are the networkers and innovators, those agents of action who make things happen. Catalysts are the classroom stars whom everyone aspires to be, the ones invited to parties to ensure excitement. Catalysts—Ralph Nader is a prime example here—are essential to society for their innovations. Catalysts generally have boundless energy and actually appear to thrive on stress. They must have an arena in which to perform, or they become morose and counterproductive.

Cause Fighter—The number of causes is infinite—peace, whales, hunger, and so on—and the cause fighter will either be drawn to them or will create more. These entities fulfill an important function by speaking for others who are perhaps too absorbed with their own themes to address social issues. Cause fighters have a tendency toward impulsiveness that can place themselves *and others* in jeopardy. It is also necessary that cause fighters consider the possibility that the cause itself is minimal compared to their ego involvement.

Controller—The challenge for this entity is obvious. Napoleon and Hitler were typical examples of this theme manifested in its most negative sense. The controller feels compelled to not only run the broad overall show, but to dictate to others how they must perform the smallest detail of their lives. In order to perfect, these entities must learn self-control and restraint.

Emotionality—Not only the euphoric highs and the devastating lows, but every subtle nuance of emotion will be felt by these entities. Frequently, emotionality is a secondary theme of poets and artists. As such, it will indeed enhance creativity while imposing a severe challenge. The recognition of a need for balance is vital here, as is the establishment of intellectual self-control.

Experiencer—It's not unusual for this entity to go from flower child to bank president to vagabond touring the world in a self-made boat. Experiencers dabble in nearly everything and master many of their pursuits. Howard Hughes is a well-known example. Wealth is merely a by-product of a multifaceted experience. Good health is essential to an experiencer; it is important not to jeopardize this by excesses.

Fallibility—These entities appear to be always at the wrong place at the wrong time, for they have entered life with a physical, mental, or emotional handicap. Helen Keller, who as an infant contracted a fever that left her deaf and blind, is an excellent example. Her triumph over these handicaps is an inspiration to everyone. It is important for entities with a fallibility theme to remember that they chose this path in order to set an example for the rest of us.

Follower—Initially, these entities might have preferred to be leaders, but on some level they decided not to make the necessary commitment. The challenge of the follower is to realize that leadership is impossible without them and so recognize their own importance. Perfection comes from accepting the self-chosen theme and providing the leader with the best support possible. Discrimination is necessary here in deciding exactly who and what to follow.

Harmony—Balance remains all-important to these entities, and they will go to any length to maintain it. Their personal sacrifices are admirable up to a point, but the real challenge lies in the acceptance of life's wrinkles. What can't be changed must be adapted to and accepted.

Healer—Entities with this theme are naturally drawn to some aspect of the healing professions, physical or mental. The good they do is obvious. The only danger is that they can easily become too empathetic. It is imperative that those with a healer theme pace themselves so that they avoid burnout.

Humanitarian—While Cause Fighters and Banner Carriers cry out against the wrongs committed against humankind, the Humanitarian theme takes these entities into the action itself. Humanitarians are too busy bandaging, teaching, holding, saving, and so on, to have time for protests. Those in this category aren't much concerned with the concept of evil, and they are inclined to excuse humankind for its faults. Since humanitarians rarely stop with family and friends, reaching far beyond to anyone and everyone who touches them, they are in danger of over-extending themselves. The challenge for the humanitarian—my challenge—is to avoid physical burnout through self-love and nourishment.

Infallibility—These entities are born rich, handsome, attractive, witty, and so forth. When we consider that perfection is the universal goal, this theme becomes one of the most challenging. There is often a tendency toward excesses of all kinds. It's almost as if the entity wants to tempt fate. Curiously, there may often be a lack of self-esteem that causes the entity to fear that he or she is not lovable as an individual. The goal here is to truly accept the theme and learn to live with it.

Intellectuality—Here is the theme of the professional student. Charles Darwin, who used the knowledge that he acquired through intensive study to experiment, hypothesize, and eventually publish, is an excellent example of one who has perfected this theme. But since knowledge for its own sake is frequently the goal among intellectuals, there is often a danger that the knowledge that has been so ardently sought and painfully acquired will go nowhere.

Irritant—Deliberate faultfinders, these entities are essential to the perfection of others, for in their company we are forced to learn patience and tolerance. Although it's important not to play into the Irritant's innate pessimism, we must also be nonjudgmental. We must remember that Irritants are perfecting their themes so that we can perfect ours through them.

Justice—Many of the Founding Fathers, concerned as they were with fairness and equality, are examples of the Justice theme in operation. Those with Justice as a theme will eagerly give their names when they've witnessed an accident or crime. As admirable as all this sounds, it is imperative that these entities use discretion in their choices. Mob violence is another misguided attempt to right a wrong. Those with Justice as a theme must remain God-centered.

Lawfulness—Practicing or teaching law are obvious choices for these entities, who are almost obsessed with issues of legality. Some of these individuals may also be found serving on governing boards. When elevated, these souls keep the world safe and balanced, but they must always be on guard against the possibility of using their power in a self-serving manner.

Leader—Those who pursue this theme are self-controlled, premeditated, and rarely innovative. They become leaders in areas that are already established. Their drive is toward success rather than creation. Their challenge is to avoid "power trips."

Loner—Although often in the vanguard of society, those with the theme of Loner invariably pick occupations or situations in which they are in some way isolated. This is a secondary theme of mine. Being a psychic has set me apart from others. Loners are generally happy with themselves but should watch their irritation levels when people come into their space. If each theme recognizes the presence and significance of other themes, the result will be far greater tolerance and understanding in the world, and—eventually—peace.

Loser—Entities with a loser theme are extremely negative, though unlike those with fallibility as a theme, they are born without handicaps. Often they have many good points, but choose to ignore them. Although their theme may resemble that of the Irritant in their proclivity for constant criticism, they are different in that they invariably place the blame back on "poor me." These entities are prime martyrs, moving from one elaborate soap opera to another. By observing this theme in action, we endeavor to be more positive. It is important that we not judge the people who have this theme, remembering that their patterns were chosen to enable us to perfect ourselves.

Manipulator—This is one of the most powerful themes, for Manipulators are easily able to control situations as well as people. By viewing people and situations as a chessboard, those with a Manipulator theme can move people and circumstance to their advantage, as though they were pawns. President Franklin Roosevelt was a prime example of a Manipulator in action. When such a person works for the good of others, this theme is elevated to its highest purpose. When the theme is misused, the ultimate goal of perfection takes a long time to achieve.

Passivity—Surprisingly, entities with a Passivity theme are actually active—but about nothing. Although they will at times take stands on issues, it is always in a nonviolent manner. Although any extreme is hurtful to the individual, *some* tension may be needed in order to bring about the perfection of the soul.

Patience—The Patience theme is clearly one of the most difficult paths to perfection. Those with this theme seem to desire a more rapid attainment of perfection than entities with less challenging themes. Often, they carry great amounts of guilt when they feel that they have strayed from their goal and become impatient. This attitude can lead to self-abasement, and sometimes lead to suppressed anger. These entities must be lenient with themselves, for it is difficult enough living through the circumstances they have chosen in order to express this theme.

Pawn—The biblical Judas is a classic example of this theme. Whether the means is negative or positive, Pawns trigger something of great magnitude into being. We cannot evolve toward universal perfection without the Pawn, but those entities who select this theme should preserve their dignity by only picking worthy causes.

Peacemaker—Entities who select the theme of Peacemaker are not as pacific as the name implies. Peacemakers are actually pushy in their desire for and pursuit of peace. They work endlessly to stop violence and war, addressing a larger audience than those who've opted for Harmony as a theme. Their goal of peace far exceeds an allegiance to one particular group or country.

Performance—Those with a Performance theme find it highly rewarding but frequently exhausting. These entities are the true "party animals." Some will go into actual entertainment careers, but others will simply be content to entertain in their homes or offices. The challenge here is for those with Performance as a theme to combat burnout by looking within, thus acquiring the ability to nourish and "entertain" themselves.

Persecution—This arduous theme is chosen to allow others to grow spiritually. Entities with a Persecution theme live their lives in anticipation of the worst, certain that they are being singled out for persecution. Experiencing pleasure can throw them into a panic because they are convinced that somehow they must pay for it.

Persecutor—Those with a Persecutor theme may range from wife beaters and child abusers to mass murderers. It's difficult to see the purpose of this theme within a single life span, but these seemingly "bad seeds" have a self-chosen role to play that enables humankind to evolve toward perfection. Once again, it is imperative that we not attempt to judge the individual.

Poverty—The theme of Poverty appears most frequently in Third World countries, yet it can be even more of a challenge in affluent societies. Some entities with Poverty as a theme may even have all they need to be comfortable and yet *feel* poor. With progress, the frenzy fades and is slowly replaced by a sense of bliss as the realization comes that the trappings of this world are transitory things whose importance will quickly pass.

Psychic—The theme of Psychic is more a challenge than a gift, at least in the early stages. An entity with this theme is able to hear, see, or sense things in a manner beyond that of natural sense perception. Often it comes to those in strict backgrounds where authority figures strive to deny or suppress the gift. Eventually, the entity will learn to accept and live with the ability, using it for good in a spiritual, if not professional, manner. Incidentally, I do not carry this theme; psychic ability has never been a challenge point in my life.

Rejection—This challenging theme manifests itself early, with rejection and alienation experienced in childhood. The syndrome accelerates with entry into school and subsequent involvement in relationships. Often these entities are deserted by those they love—even their own children will adopt surrogate mother or father figures. The pattern can be broken once the entity recognizes what is happening and surrenders the action and the ego involvement to God.

Rescuer—One often finds the Rescuer working alongside the Cause Fighter, but when the Cause Fighter moves on to another cause, the Rescuer remains to care for the victim. Even when the victims have obviously created their own problems, the Rescuer is determined to "save" them. Often, in so doing, it is the Rescuer who is victimized. An entity with a Rescuer theme has a high degree of empathy and can manifest strength for those in need. This theme presents a tough road to travel, but the spiritual rewards are great indeed.

Responsibility—Individuals who have chosen the Responsibility theme embrace it with fervor rather than obligation, and feel guilty if they don't take care of everyone who comes into their orbit. The challenge is to decide what is immediate and necessary and then to stand back and allow others to share in the assumption of responsibilities.

Spirituality—The quest to find a spiritual center is all-encompassing for entities pursuing the Spirituality theme. When the full potential of this theme has been reached, these entities are far-sighted, compassionate, and magnanimous, but while still involved in the search, these entities must guard against being narrow and judgmental in their views.

Survival—For any number of reasons, real or imagined, life is a constant struggle for those who've selected a Survival theme. At their best in a crisis situation, these souls take a grim view of day-to-day existence. The obvious challenge here is to lighten up.

Temperance—Very probably, the entity with a Temperance theme is dealing with an addiction of one kind or another. The challenge here is to avoid extremes. Perhaps the entity has conquered the actual addiction but is still dealing with a residue of feelings about it. The key to combating the fanaticism that often characterizes those with Temperance as a theme is moderation—the true meaning of temperance.

Tolerance—Entities choosing the tolerance theme must be tolerant about everything—world affairs, relatives, children, politics, and so forth. The burden is so great that they often will only choose one area to tolerate, remaining very narrow-minded to all the rest. By recognizing their theme, these entities can meet the challenge and so grow more and more magnanimous.

Victim—These entities have chosen to be martyrs and sacrificial lambs. By their example—dramatically displayed by the media—we are made aware of injustice. Jack Kennedy is an example of one pursuing a Victim theme—not merely his means of exit, but his back pain, his family name, and the pressures placed upon him by his parents. Many Victims, after having played their parts, may choose to rewrite future scripts by altering their masochistic tendencies.

Victimizer—People's Temple leader Jim Jones was a prime example of the Victimizer theme in action. Within the framework of one's own viewpoint of life, it is almost impossible to see the full purpose of Jones's manifestation of this theme, yet it is obvious that many lives, as well as many life themes, interacted with his. In the tapestry of life, Jones's unique role may have been to focus public attention on cult abuses.

Warrior—Entities with a Warrior theme are fearless risk takers who assume a variety of physical challenges. Many go into some form of military service or law enforcement. With Humanitarian as a secondary theme, they may be particularly effective. Although it is important to temper aggression, it still remains that without Warriors, we would be prey to tyrants.

Wealth—This theme sounds like a great choice, but invariably it is more like a burden and leads to destructive behaviors if unchecked. As always, the goal of a theme is to overcome the negative aspects, and Wealth is a seductive tempter that acts like an addiction—it is very difficult to gain control of this theme, and it usually becomes one's master. People will be obsessed with acquiring wealth, growing it, and hoarding it. They will not be concerned with the methods of acquisition nor the consequences of their actions in their quest for more. Moral values are of no importance to this theme. Usually it takes many lives to overcome due to its powerful effect on a person.

When people do finally master Wealth, then you find them freely giving away their belongings, with no desire for anything in return.

Winner—Unlike those entities with Infallibility as a theme, to whom everything comes easily, Winners feel compelled to achieve. They strive to win with great tenacity, often gambling or entering contests. Perennial optimists, they are always certain that the next deal, the next job, even the next marriage will be the best. No sooner has one deal fallen through than they pick themselves up and go on to what they know will be a winning situation. Present Eisenhower was a positive example of this theme. As a general, his unfailing optimism was inspiring; as a president, his confidence had a calming effect. The challenge for these entities—which Eisenhower appears to have met—is to take a realistic approach to winning.

Our Origins

Francine: Never think that at the "end of the world" we will all be absorbed into a nebulous, cosmic mind that is all one. That image only applies to God, who has no beginning or end. However, from the very "beginning" of your inception, you had a definite and unique purpose. You will always be a defined, singular part of the Divine. As you began to migrate through life's schooling processes, being the experiencing and emotional part of God, karma was born.

In one lifetime, you go through your garden of Eden, your purgatory, your hells, and then, of course, your heavens. Even a small child who exits at an early age goes through versions of these stages.

If you look at the Bible as a chronicle of your movement through life, you'll have your Adam and Eve period, your Exodus period, your time in the Desert, your time of Rebirth, and your Resurrection. All the parts of the Bible really relate to your journey. You will be tempted. You will have the sorrows of Job. You will be a prophet—all the aspects. You will be king of all you survey. You will be a slave to all you survey. Can you fit all of that into seven lifetimes, let's say? You could get it into one or two, if you so chose. Many choose at least ten—some less, some many more.

If you're around a person who's just beginning their cycle, and you're almost on your last, you really won't be able to tolerate them. It has nothing to do with the fact that you're more evolved. For example, when you see young teenage boys and girls giggling and laughing, do you know why you can't stand it? Because you can remember, consciously or not, how silly you were. But you will always say, "When I was that age, I was never that silly."

Jesus asked, "Why hast Thou forsaken me?" He was purposely revealing his own humanity, showing that there can be despair. His life, as well as other Biblical examples, reflect times of despair, times of triumph, and times of Passover. Jesus, in his one life, really presented a whole spectrum of what others might do in many lives.

I know Jesus very well, as all of you do when you're on my side. I can tell you that he seemingly *did* despair. It was a bit of an angry outcry: "Where are You? What are You doing?" All of us have asked this: "Are You really up there? Do You care enough to know what's going on with me?" This showed that anyone can really get downright angry with the Creator, and it's all right.

If you look at Jesus very closely, you will see that he fulfilled all 45 themes that humanity is working through. In the same way, if you look at the Bible as one person's yearning and struggle through their lifetimes, then it's much more understandable. That person spent time in the desert, had a mission, and had a time of prophecy.

You constantly go through rebirth and death. When you finally leave that shell behind, you should go beyond that cycle, and do not form other shells. When you first started in this cycle, you were almost like Adam and Eve—terribly naive, believing, and caring. Then life began to hurt everyone, no matter how evolved they were. You had a choice to come in again and either work through your theme, endure more hurt, or put on more overlays of behavior.

Eventually you come to some type of plateau, where you begin to take the overlays off but remain more evolved—back to the Adam and Eve stage again, *with the naiveté, but with strength and conviction*. It's like starting out as a child, becoming too sophisticated, and having to go back to simplicity again.

That's why Jesus' words were so profound when he said that those who were like children would understand. We start out as children, then become very sophisticated and hardened through living—and then, lo and behold, we have to drop it all, hopefully with greater courage, insight, awareness, and simplicity than we ever had before.

Notice that almost all of the great people in the world had a tremendous childlike quality, high intellect, and great forgiveness of heart. The more adult we think we've become, the more we think we can deal in a sophisticated manner with life. We think that we're beyond hurt, becoming hardened, embittered, cruel, vindictive, sarcastic, and hateful. That only means that you have a shell around you that is so hard that it's literally making your soul raw.

In your lifetime, try to get just four people to stand with you and really say that they love you and you love them. It is like the "12 wise or good men" syndrome. Certainly a mother who has four children will say, "I have four I love." But she can't always count on them just because they're related. They will grow up to live their own lives. Please get out of the habit of loving because you "must."

Please remember that no soul is so evolved that they're beyond childlike behavior. Part of the reason there's so much derangement in your society is that you're not allowed to act like willful children. No one tolerates the behavior patterns of others for very long. If you're constantly depressed, you must for your own soul's sake learn to check yourself every day. This is not going to make you overzealous about yourself; it's going to make you aware and loving of yourself.

Check yourself when you get up. If you have a slow metabolism, say to yourself first, "How do I feel today? Do I feel depressed? Do I feel fair, good, excellent?" If you don't feel good, then say to yourself, "It might not be an excellent day, but it will become a good day." It will not happen at first, but what really makes a day good? What really makes a lifetime good? Not the circumstances, but the way you view it.

Three people can watch a death. One person says, "Why did she leave?" The next person has anger. The other person may say, "Thank God she's gone." No one person is right or wrong about their evaluation. Each is at a different level of understanding.

The longer you live, hopefully, the more you will *not* grow up. Be more childlike. Be more simplistic. The aging process has a way of doing that, but too often it is misclassified as senility, doddering around, whining, being forgetful, and drooling food out of one's mouth. But some elderly people, instead, become childlike, almost as if they've come full circle; they look at everything as being mysterious, wonderful, and new. They begin to remember, understand, and see everything through different eyes once again.

The Other Side is far more beautiful than anything you have here, but returning to Earth is like going back to your old school. There is a sense of attachment to Earth, although it's not nearly as beautiful. It's a reflected place, shadowy at best, but still containing its own beauty.

If you were black in your prior life, wouldn't it be a marvel to look at your hand and see white skin, or vice versa? Do you ever watch how babies stare when they see themselves in a mirror? What's even more amazing is that some babies will even act like they're looking at another baby. They don't even recognize themselves.

You say, "Well, why would they? They have little bitty minds, and they're not smart yet." But they are. That soul is alive in there, with intellect and all the inductive and deductive reasoning from every lifetime and from the Other Side. The brain is not fully connected yet, but that soul is aware behind those little eyes.

Babies are not blank slates, but suddenly they're immersed in new things—you're putting new fingerprints, new input, all over them. It may be a tremendously different world time for them. Say they were last here in medieval times, and all of a sudden they find themselves in the 20th century. It will be totally different.

When do we lose memory of past lives?

They begin to fade at about four years of age—from two to four, they're very clear. If children can talk prior to age two, it's amazing what they can tell you.

Older children use dreams to remember because they're not yet bogged down with overlays. Children raised in open-minded homes, which accept the truth of reincarnation, will not hesitate to talk about it. You send out the vibration of acceptance. Everyone carries all that knowledge with them, even if they never mention it.

You're going to have children who convert telepathic communications into dreams, transmitting and receiving. Encourage the children to discuss their vision, dreams, and insights. You have another chance to do this with grandchildren, which is even more important. No one ever thinks to ask a child, "What were you before?" as Sylvia has suggested so many times.

Mothers will say, "They never told me." But did you ever ask them? Try it: "Where were you before? Where did you live before?" They will answer you; mothers have heard these stories for years. It's not just imagination. A child will get up in the morning and say, "I went fishing last night." The mother will say, "Oh, it was just a dream."

Be very careful about saying that everything is a dream. They could be visiting the Other Side. There's a lot of soul travel back and forth; that's why babies jerk so much. Did you ever watch a baby breathe and jerk? They're in and out of their body very quickly all the time. It's almost as if the soul is getting fitted to the body.

Babies' eyes will roll back in their heads. They will make all kinds of funny little squeaky noises—jerking, jumping, and wiggling. For the new mother, it's quite frightening. They moan; they roll around. It's awfully hard for that soul to become accustomed to the body again.

What causes crib death?

Crib death happens when entities come in, but then they decide that they don't want to stay, so then they leave. They simply depart their body and decide they're not going to come back. The same with miscarriage. It's an early form of retraction. They figure that if they do it early, it's better for all concerned.. The soul never enters the fetus in this case.

Now, you might wonder about the karma or guilt of the mother. Everything is intertwined. That child chose to come into life, and to negate its life. This is always due to conditions being wrong for that soul's perfection, or for the experience value learned by the family.

Knowing and experiencing are two different things. Most of you chose to come down in rapid succession. That's good, because you get it over with quickly, but it's also tremendously tiring. The soul becomes very worn out from it.

We have a tendency, even on my side, to "know better." Please don't feel that we're all like cheerful Pollyannas over on my side. We don't have egos as you know them. We're truly centered within our "I Am." However, certainly we have conflicts, arguments, likes, and dislikes.

I can't imagine anything more boring than to live all your life with your individual personality—your purposes, your likes, your temperament—and all of a sudden come over to my side and lose all that flavor. Not only would you not be yourself anymore, but you'd be an android.

On my side, we see tempers flare; we can see auras flare. At controversial lectures, I've seen people argue, and I could see the flaring auras. Maybe there's no one resolution of the way two people think, but there are never fist fights or vicious acts. There is disagreement and debate without needing a "winner."

Sylvia, for instance, as I have said many times, was not close to me on the Other Side. We've become close in this life, but she really wasn't part of the group I was with. In fact, at one point, Sylvia thought I was cold and aloof. She may have been right. I found her to be almost too exuberant, much like a puppy. So, your dispositions may not match socially, but they do well for a given job.

You can tell, by people's behavior, how much in their life they fit the patterns of extroversion and introversion. There are a lot of introverts who are really very quiet, introverted people, and they're not blocked at all. *Shy* is a better word. Then you'll find another type of so-called introverts who are actually blocked, cold, hostile, and standoffish. This is not introverted, but blocked.

On the Other Side, we allow each one of us to simply be. That's why you have a hard time with egos on your plane. Your mind remembers where everyone got along well. When there was tremendous intellectual enthusiasm, euphoric highs, and marvelous feelings of, "What will the next thing be." There is a total enjoyment of loved ones and yourself.

On your plane, you have to fight to find any enjoyment at all. No one seems to understand you, and you don't get them either. You can't be assured of reliable communication. It takes far too many words to convey your thoughts.

Even with these words I'm now uttering, there are many levels on which you can receive me, many levels of understanding. That's why you get so confused. Yet, how do you get things across?

If your motive is in the right place, don't be so cautious with your spoken words. Consider this: Why do certain words make you mad one time, and yet the same words can be laughed off at another time? It depends on how you accept it. I've seen some of you. When someone speaks negatively, you just smile and walk away. A friend will grab you and say, "Did you hear that?" You just smile or change the subject, but your "busybody" friend says, "Well, if they'd said that to me, I'd be furious." Then they go on to explain to you why *you* should be furious.

Be true to your own truth, not another's opinion. By doing the latter, you're being manipulated into action. People do this to their spouses and friends all the time. Married couples, too, often get dragged down into competing over who rules the household. Yet any true ruler never has to say one word about it. The minute a man says, "I wear the pants around here," people know that he probably doesn't have any on at all. The minute a woman says that she rules the roost, she exhibits the same flaring insecurity. The truth is that no one rules any home. You rule in separate areas. No one should try to master anyone; be partners instead.

If a negative situation between two people does occur, then one has barked and the other one has gone into the submissive role. Not for one minute does anyone actually have mastery over another. A king may have authority, but the slave knows that no one can rule their soul. That is one of the messages that Moses tried to get across.

The Purpose of Life Themes

As Sylvia mentioned previously, you all came in with both a primary and a secondary theme. One theme you work *with,* and the other (usually the secondary theme) you have to work *through.* That is the one that will cause you the most problems.

Let's say that your primary theme is Humanitarian. That's something that you simply *are* and it flows easily. The secondary theme may be Tolerance. That's the one you have to push against and overcome; it will hold you up and rub against you like coarse wool. There's always one that's more harsh.

If your themes are Activator and Harmony, then Activator is the harshest one, which you have to modify, control, calm down, and work through. It makes it much simpler. Of course, you would not want to work through Harmony.

Usually, in every set of themes, there's a positive and a negative. The two contrasts rub together. You wouldn't want to rebel against being a Humanitarian. Let's say your themes were Humanitarian and Activator, and you chose to become a hermit. You would then be rubbing against both your themes, and you could go totally off-track. Nothing in those two themes lends itself to your being a solitary person.

Most of you have *active* themes that, by their very character, will force you out. Even the Pawn theme is active, because Pawns place themselves in position. The Tolerance theme is much more quiet, but even that will actively force you into positions in which you have to be tolerant. Both the Experiencer and Humanitarian themes demand that the person be out in front of others. You never find a Humanitarian sitting on a mountaintop contemplating their navel—there's no way. They will be out and doing something.

Your theme will rise up—either in this life or another. Long before you ever knew what your themes were, you activated them. The only difference is that when you get to a certain level, you begin to understand. There is a certain purpose or drive within your life that pushes you forward to complete some goal. That's why human beings down through the centuries have said, "What is my purpose? What am

I here for? What am I perfecting?"

The ultimate pinnacle of that is to *perfect for God*. It's certainly better to *know* what your theme, purpose, and goal is than to just walk blindly through life.

Let's say that someone was an Activator and a Humanitarian, and decided to take themselves away to a monastery—it's rare, but it does happen. They would find that they were being constantly reprimanded for talking, and helping another person. It would soon appear to them, or should, that they are in the *wrong* position. That's why in life, you have to constantly monitor where you are. Life has no guarantees that everything will be fair and that there will be no failures.

There is, however, a guarantee that you will find—not necessarily inner peace—but certainly, inner happiness. Happiness comes from the conviction of knowing you're doing the *right* thing regardless of what your culture, religion, or society says.

So many times human beings have to be pushed to the point of desperation, whether it relates to illness, fatigue, or despair, before they realize that they're not in the right field. You must start to decide. Your work situation may not be fun. If you aren't getting some inner happiness out of it, then you're off-track by staying in that place. Do *not* absorb the feelings of people around you, because they can be miserable.

If you're a teacher, nurse, bookkeeper, or in a technical field—and inside you there's a feeling of completion, challenge, helping, and doing—then at least part of your theme *is* being fulfilled. But if every day at work or in a relationship, it comes to such a point of misery that your inner God-center is saying that you're wrong, then you're *not* following the path.

Let's go even deeper into the victimization. When a person begins to feel like they're a bleeding, wounded, despairing *victim,* their theme then has been aborted. There are days and weeks in which they'll go on with a marriage, relationship, or situation and become more dire and more despairing. Their theme, then, has gotten lost in this dark forest of pain.

The theme of Victim doesn't mean that throughout your whole life you must be victimized. Please believe me—every minute of your life at work, at home, or anywhere else won't be a cake walk, but what if it becomes one endless nightmare of pain and arduous living? Then there's something wrong. Let's say you have no job and no companion, but within yourself you find your journey in aloneness arduous. Then the alarm system within you is saying, "Change steps."

Even a small step gets you out of the gutter. People think that they can't make things better, because that entails going back and undoing or changing. They think that children must love them, or they must make a huge effort to make the bend in the road not so sharp. By changing a friendship or moving from one place to another—even as minimal a change as moving your bed to a different spot in a room—you can create a more pleasant atmosphere. Even change the colors that you wear, or your hairstyle.

Notice that when people start getting depressed, the first thing they let go of is their personal appearance. They no longer take pride in it, and such lack of pride was looked on for many years as being honorable.

We find this in your religions, don't we? Everything is to be hooded and covered. The minute a woman entered the nunnery, her hair and her finery was covered. This was to cut down self-esteem and create a *nonentity* approach to life. Dress people in uniforms constantly, cover them over so no one sees them, and they all become autonomous entities who lose their identity. That's how so many of your businesses, religions, and social structures operate.

There's something in the human being that wants acceptance. That's why fads constantly spread. Whether the fad is long or short hair, everybody wears it, even if it makes them look ridiculous. At the root, it's a longing for the Other Side, where everyone feels accepted. On the Other Side, there is total acceptance. On Earth, you suffer from extreme homesickness.

When you look in the mirror, look with an eye toward loving yourself and perfecting your theme. Don't look through the eyes of some awful spouse or parent, or someone who has hurt you. Don't fall into that pattern, although it's all too easy if someone has been oppressive to you, like a mother who has called you stupid, ugly, or dumb. Many times when you look in the mirror, you see the picture that the person has put on you. Reject it.

Instead, look with your soul's eyes. Say to God, "I want to look in the mirror with my own soul's eyes. I want to see myself shining." Do not look at the aging process or at what life has done—use the inner eyes to see the beauty of your soul. Don't worry so much if you've gained extra pounds or if your hair's gotten a little drab. Your soul isn't affected. Focus on the beauty within and the feeling that your spark of the Divine is gorgeous beyond words.

Start going through your theme very specifically, asking, "Am I living up to it?" I want you to get the most out of this life without having to come back. If your theme is Warrior, that does *not* mean that you're going to take sword in hand and go charging around. But it does mean that, whether you like it or not, you'll want to fight for things. That does *not* mean that you have to enlist in the army. Warriors and Cause Fighters are very similar. Warriors stand and fight for what's right. They are the ones whose hands raise up when they perceive an injustice.

The more you get into the depths of your last life, you start picking up bits and pieces of *all* the other themes. Certainly the major theme stands out clearly because there are many lifetimes of that. But when a person is finished with that, they're allowed to pick any number of themes to enhance their true self.

Look at this as courses of study in school. You took algebra, geometry, and then calculus. You take progressively harder courses. Why? You wanted to graduate with higher honors. Now there's no penalty if you happen to attempt a theme that you simply can't perfect. That's all right, because you've already completed your major and minor theme anyway—although that theme still rears its head every once in a while.

That's why many people say, "I thought that old part of my life was dead, and here that pattern comes again." Many patterns are linked to your theme. Let's say you're a Victim: Once you realize that every person that you've met has victimized you, then it stops.

What you must do is *change tracks*. People ask, "How can I do that at my age?" What does age matter? If you're 50 or 60 and you decide to go back to school, that's marvelous. How many people have gone back to school at 55 and graduated at 59? Or become a doctor or priest? Let me tell you something: When a person does that, their chances of a longer and happier life are ten times greater than a 30-year-old in a miserable life. You need the joy of living, the joy of what' is around the next corner.

If you feel that you want to do something new right now, that's a *sure sign* that you're burnt out and you ought to change. You ask, "How could I possibly change when I have no money?" Well, you'll change if you end up in the hospital! That's a sure way to get you to put an end to a way of life that's no longer healthy for you.

We may spend our whole life doing something we hate just to make a lot of money, because society told us we should. Or we feel that it's the only thing we know how to do. We're too afraid to switch.

What if you feel that you're not skilled enough to do anything? Then go out and learn a skill. Of course your physical body is tired and lazy—this is the biggest problem that you have to fight against, aside from your theme. The mind tries to go faster, but your body won't move. It's not your fault. Be patient with it as it accustoms itself to a new challenge.

Were themes distributed equally? Did we have a choice?

No, to the first question; and, yes, you did choose your themes. If a group of entities all chose Humanitarian, that doesn't mean that they will all come down at once. They wouldn't necessarily come down during the Dark Ages, but rather, whenever there is much chaos and many horrific dark entities, in order to fight for humanity.

Those with the theme of Victim would come down during the Dark Ages and the Inquisition, because those times would be optimal for that theme. So you'll see defined times in which a great majority of one theme will come down, and hardly any of another.

At present, we're seeing a lot of the following themes: Humanitarian, Harmony, Experiencer, and Activator. You'll find them in clumps. The quieter, more sedentary themes came in around A.D. 1100 when there were a lot of monastic, spiritual, scholarly lives. When there's a war, then you'll see the more aggressive themes such as Winner and Warrior. They will all come down in the best time that fits their theme.

On Earth now, we can find virtually every theme, because you have every possible horror in any part of the world you want to go to. You have themes clashing against themes. We do not clash on the Other Side.

I find it so amazing that people ask each others what their "sign" is. They should ask about their *theme*. Harmony goes well with Humanitarian, but neither of those go with Cause Fighter or Warrior. The latter two would be a tempestuous relationship. Persecutor and Victim would be wonderful together.

Could we wisely choose themes before we had experience?

That's when you *did* choose them. In your "alwaysness," you chose from the very beginning. Just as you know that you are basically a male or a female entity, which you knew from the very "beginning," so, too, did you know your path to perfection. You might have waited around, hesitated, and worked on the Other Side for a long time first, but you eventually began incarnating.

The only way we can ever perfect is to get down here and work through it. I chose to be a communicating guide instead of coming back into life. I'm not sure I didn't choose the wrong thing.

Can we have incompatible themes?

Yes—consider the paradox of Sylvia's Humanitarian-Loner themes: "I would love to be alone, but I'm forced out into the public eye." People with this theme combination always have a sense of aloneness about them, yet they're always giving out to everyone else.

Is every obstacle planned in our chart?

Sometimes, as we watch things happen, we say, "Wait a minute, something's wrong. That wasn't charted here." Yet, ultimately, in the overall picture, it *was*. Darkness can descend without our conscious knowledge, because dark entities follow no chart. They can randomly hit anywhere they want and wreak havoc with a chart. It's like you're going down the highway and a big hailstorm hits. The hailstorm was not charted, and it won't make you run off the road, but what a mess it is to get through. The minute you come into life, the dark entities can take random shots at you.

Sometimes you go in and out of your major theme. You'll invest lots of time in which you're really focusing on it. You're faced with one situation after another. Then all of a sudden, nothing happens for a while, and you think you're not fulfilling your chart.

The tragedy with most human beings is that they don't know how to relax. They think if they're not activating or not saving the world, then they're not doing anything. Yet, please realize that boredom in itself can be a test.

Can we stop following our themes?

No, you cannot. That is the thrust and purpose of your life.

Can you say a little more about the Pawn and Catalyst themes.

Pawns are like Catalysts; they're always the steps upon which other people climb. They're the ones who hold their hand out so someone else can get a footing somewhere. If you watch Pawns come in, they always have people revolving around them, in the same way that Catalysts do.

Pawns are not as activated as Catalysts. Pawns are there to make something happen, but they're never around to see it finish so they don't get as much satisfaction as a Catalyst does. Pawns have to be tolerant and patient. If one person is a Catalyst and another is a Pawn, they'll get along well together. However, being a Pawn is not bad—they're the ones who take positions for others to perfect. Of course they get used, but I think everybody in life does. Pawns are certainly used for a greater good, though.

The Catalyst theme differs in that they will take just so much of being caught in between all the action. Then they've had enough—and they simply step aside for the other parties to continue. Catalysts say, "Let's hurry up and get everything done."

What about the Activator?

That person must always be busy doing something, whether it's mentally, physically, or spiritually. They must feel like they're starting new projects all the time, but they don't ever finish them.

Compare Tolerance and Patience.

Tolerance means you have to endure oppression of every type. It can be as simple as tolerating the dispositions of everyone around you, or just tolerating yourself. Patience means you have to allow others to take precedence over you. Patience is much less traumatic than Tolerance.

What does Builder-Catalyst entail?

A Catalyst causes something to happen. A Builder creates a situation for another person to build their life upon. The only tragedy that a Builder has to face is that they usually lay down all the groundwork, and then somebody else runs away with the honors.

What about the Rejection theme?

Those with this theme have a tendency to draw from every aspect of life: feeling rejected, being rejected, wanting to reject, and then wanting everything good so they won't be rejected by it. A fully entrenched life could find rejection from parents, siblings, schoolmates, co-workers, mates, and children. This is a very tough theme for any soul to perfect.

The more negative the theme, the *more* the soul wants to perfect it fast to get finished. Only very brave souls will pick negative themes. Highly evolved souls are going to pick negative themes because they're meant to *overcome* their theme. It does *not* go on forever. Once an individual recognizes the pattern, then they can be done with it.

What we're supposed to do is survive life in spite of our themes.

Please talk about Banner Carriers.

They are like Cause Fighters, but they use verbalization and demonstration to support a cause. They march in the front line of a new cause, get lots of people riled up, then slip away to a different cause.

Can Cause Fighters create causes?

Oh, they do. If they can't find something to fight for, they may well invent a new cause and then clean it up afterwards. Fortunately, this world has more than enough causes to keep them very busy.

What is the Warrior theme about?

A Warrior is a very warlike entity who wants to be involved in a fight on some level. The obvious occupations for Warriors are the military and police work. But they will also show up for important political, social, and religious issues, too. Warrior is similar to Activist, but the Warrior will take a fight to a higher, even physical, level.

What about the Passive theme?

It's almost in direct opposition to Warrior. The theme of Passive seems to be awfully ominous. It's actually something to work through, as are Loner and Pawn. If you came in with a lot of things you wanted to do, and yet circumstances block you every time, then you must learn to accept your fate.

What about the theme of Justice?

If you have this theme, it's the key to your whole life. The final testing of this comes at your last exit point; you will then know, with all assuredness, that you fulfilled enough "points" along the way and bettered your theme. However, not every circumstance in your life can be attributed to theme development. A lot of things are just so much trivia, without significant impact.

Maybe you weren't supposed to break a foot, but that option existed. If you took the option to break your foot, then you might have done so simply to get rest, or to get into the hospital and create harmony between two people who were fighting.

You will never get away from your theme. It will always rise up in front of you. For most people, they want no involvement when others are quarreling, but a Harmony/Justice person would say, "It *is* my business, because it's *bothering* me."

What are your themes, Francine?

My themes have always been Winner and Activator. Winner was the hard one for me. Born in an Aztec community as a young woman under male dominance, there was nowhere I could win. So it was just as well that I died at 19.

Did I carry my theme to my side? Yes, you bet I did. We carry our themes to the ultimate, then, with nothing to hold us back and no one thinking that we're being egotistical, we become individually bright and shining. The negative side of the theme drops away when you come to the Other Side.

I see so many of you living lives of quiet desperation with spouses whom you don't care about, children who hurt you, jobs that are just horrifying, and the feeling that there's no relief. *Please stop.* One woman read Sylvia's biography, stopped everything she was doing in her life, and started designing T-shirts. She had never had faith that she could do it, and now her designs are everywhere. It was daunting for her to leave her job and security and say, "I must do what I've always wanted to do." As soon as she opened up her hands to God and gave up the so-called security, she met someone in marketing who gave her a chance and who's now displaying her works.

When you're on track, you're not supposed to be terribly miserable. Now, this doesn't mean that you suddenly find Mr./Ms. Right or that money will fall on you from heaven. But there will be a certain contentment and a quiet peace, letting God take control of your life.

Why are you so fearful of letting God steer your boat? Do you think He's blindfolded? The Mother and the Father are not blind. She can guide your boat anyplace you want, but give Her the wheel. You cannot cling to the wheel and say, "Thy will be done." This is actually a fearful phrase. It seems to take the will away from you, as if your will were different from God's. That is an impossibility, because you are *a part* of God.

Do animals have a theme?

They have a personality aspect, rather than a theme. Anyone who has animals knows that each has its own distinct personality. In that way, they're acting out their own persona. Sylvia's dog, Flower, has her own personality—she thinks she's a cat, acts like a cat, likes to wear herself around Sylvia's neck. She is totally of her *own* personality.

It is the same in nature. Even birds have distinct and different personalities. They can be mean, cranky, obstinate, fun, or clowns. Even elephants and gorillas—any beasts in the wild—have different personalities.

What data are animals sending back to God?

The facet of their personality and experiences. All this is part of God's collective consciousness. Even the way a plant grows is data to God. God is learning from every single part of how you fix your house, how you drive your car, how you wear your clothes, what you decorate with. All that is data, even from the ants that build anthills.

Themes are exclusively for humans because we have free will and choice. Even extraterrestrials are here to experience for God. This whole gigantic mass is experiencing for God. I think the extraterrestrials believe that most Earth beings are on a very low level, because most of them are very high-level entities.

It all becomes a gigantic chain of reactions. Has God had enough? There is never enough. That is infinity. That is eternity. Experience continues even on the Other Side. Knowledge is constantly growing. If God got to the point that His experiencing part became static, He would not be in the process of growth, nor would we.

That's why we choose to keep growing. Some stop—don't get me wrong. But most of us want to keep learning and experiencing for God. It becomes an addiction, believe me. The wonders within God are more glorious than I could ever tell you.

Knowledge is no substitute for experience. I could sit for hours and tell you about an experience, but you still haven't done it, have you? Each person is an individual spark of God, so each experiences things entirely differently.

Does the cycle of Earth lives end?

Of course. Then we continue to experience on the Other Side. If you choose to, you may go to other universes for experience. You never lose the experiences you have garnered. Being a part of God, you become more like God each time you experience for Him. You elevate yourself to become *like* God. That is the beauty. What you're aspiring to is not to *be* God, but to be *partners* with God.

When you first started out, even though you were totally content on the Other Side, when you came into Life, you started discovering pieces of yourself that were incomplete. You must work on each piece every time you come into life. You have to go searching through the ruins of yourself to expose those weaknesses. That's part of your quest—almost as if you dropped a precious jewel somewhere in the world and you have to find it again. You have to retrieve it. When you find that jewel, there's a tremendous happiness inside, but that doesn't mean that life will cease to knock you around.

Set your sites on a mission that's beyond a human being. It can be anything, but don't set your sights on just another human being.

That's a wasted journey. Try to make the world better. To make God come into people's hearts. To help your fellow human being. That's the goal. If someone chooses to walk with you and become a kindred spirit, then all the better. If not, then you must walk on. Drop those people who criticize your path. You will, anyway, regardless of what I say, or anyone else. You know why? A "gold ring" will appear, shining in the sky as a beacon, calling you to fulfill your chart.

The first thing you know, you'll begin your journey, and that "slug" person holding you back will not be with you anymore. Their dream is not your dream. Your ultimate wish is to perfect for God, survive life, and go Home. While you're going along the road with your eye on the beautiful gold ring, this perfect circle of eternity, help somebody else along the road. However, don't let them pull you *off* the road.

People become obsessed with one solitary focus in this life. Let's say your focus was one particular human being whom you wanted more than anything else in the world. You let everything pass because of that. How shallow that is. You will get older, you will die, that person will die, and what good came of your obsession?

How do themes relate to option lines?

The option line refers to one area of your life that you have not clearly defined in your chart; it is left open. Then you also have an emotion you must work on. It's a key to perfecting your theme. You have your theme, your option line, and your emotion to work on. Then you have your dharma, which is your responsibility to God. The option line will block a lot of people in areas such as family life, spirituality, love life, or finances. A lot of times, the option line is the very one that rubs against your theme.

For example, Sylvia's themes are Humanitarian and Loner. Her option line—which she has never been able to get control of, is her family life. This rubs directly against her Humanitarian theme.

Anytime you keep banging up against a problem, just open your hands and give it all to God. Let Him control your life. Don't be afraid that you'll get lazy and just lie there. The very fact that you worry about this means that you would never do such a thing anyway. You are actively asking for God to take control—there's the difference.

❦ Chapter Four ❦

SYNERGISM

Raheim: I want to talk to you about the progression of your soul. This process is very simple, singular, and controlled. I also want to talk to you about synergism. In your world, where two and two is four, when you apply synergism, it can become five or six because of the visualization techniques and the belief factor.

I don't intend to philosophize heavily. I want to give you the truest form of knowledge about how Gnosticism is built. When a group of people have in their mind an objective or a goal for the betterment of everyone—a belief that stretches far beyond what common reason dictates—that is synergistic. I'm not speaking of materialistic goals, which many religions focus on.

Let's say you wish to build a temple of religious worship for yourself. If this were a materialistic goal, it would have been accomplished many years ago. But because, in actuality, you are the salvation of yourself, it becomes a realistic goal.

We're not only talking about an external temple, but, more important, your personal temple. Your body is a holy temple, carrying a spark of the Divine; your actions are how you worship God.

Within the temple that is you, there should be a caring for children, compassion for the elderly, love for the downtrodden, anger against infamy, self-righteousness against wrongs, and a battle against lies. You are your temple. Synergistically, then, from your temple, which is unique, there will grow an extension into a larger temple of belief.

Whether a temple is physically built is of very little consequence. Certainly it doesn't need to be a Vatican. But before a true temple is ever built, or a society is brought about, the temple of the human being must be respected at all costs. No one individual should take precedence over another. Of course, in this day and age, there are avatars, messengers, channels, mediums, and prophets, none of whom are more holy than you are. Your meditative practices should focus on the dignity of yourself, and tolerance for the humanistic qualities of others.

If you don't care for a personal friend, a family member, a child, or a parent who defames your temple, you don't necessarily have to eradicate that person. But you must move the essence of you away from them because it stops your temple from growing.

The word that must issue from you, whoever you may be, is that you're a walking, practicing Gnostic, raising your consciousness, seeking and finding answers.

All these truths have been here but hidden from you. This was to gain control over people for as long as the world has been around. I, Raheim, may have a larger truth than you, but I will share it freely so that we're equals. In doing that, *you become avatars.*

"Saints" are highly overrated. Some took up the lance from the very beginning to come in as Cause Fighters, Banner Carriers, or prophets. They're not more holy than you are. No clergyman is more holy than you are. Do not demean yourself. You may be seekers of truth, but once you gain the truth, like Socrates or Plato, then you become equal to the mentor.

Begin to visualize and understand your perfection. Stop the wheel of life that turns continually until it grinds you up in little pieces, until you have so many behavioral overlays that you can't walk anymore. Rise out of yourself. Know that you're a spark of the Divine—blessed, beautiful, and perfect in your essence.

Any "wrongdoing" that you've done is part of the role that you've had to play. I don't mean to give you any indication that you're not responsible for your own actions, but this planet is a negative plane where hate travels faster than love.

Everything in your chart is written, as Sylvia has told you, but there is lateral movement. Each one of you is your own keeper. Each one of you enacts your own karmic retribution. Karma, as we have already stated, is the soul's experiencing for itself. But what you don't realize fully is that you built in audits and checkpoints for yourself. In other words, if you should get off-track, you will run up against someone with a message that will help restore your vision.

Life is filled with irritations. Each day that you live is a test of your theme. These tests do *not* mean you can fail. The only way that you know that you have gone through a test, and learned it, is if you can breathe a sigh of relief—if you know in your heart that you're right—no matter how hurt you may be.

Now you may say to me, "I can become so emotional that I don't know if I'm right or not." The very fact that you say to yourself in a state of emotion, "Am I doing the right thing?" shows that you are. Those who are not, don't care. If you did nothing more than ask yourself every day, "Am I on-track?" then you're spiritually advancing.

The only part of you that may not be ready to seek perfection is your insecurity, but that's cured by total commitment. If you're totally committed and you keep walking down this steep road, it will be given to you. The fact that you're on the road shows, both to the God-center within you and the God without, that at least you want to be on-track, no matter how blindly you may travel your path. It will be given to you.

The road to perfection is long and hard. Life is difficult; there is no road without both hills and ruts. There is no road without pain and sorrow. If you should ever happen to meet someone who's had a perfect life—and I doubt you ever will—they could possibly be on a "rest life." Or they don't know how bad things are because they came into this life in a numb state as a result of severe trauma from another life.

That's the most common reason for mental or physical handicaps—it's not a punishment. Rather, that person chose to incarnate in a less functional state and have people care for them, because in the preceding life, they were bludgeoned to pieces. So at least they're here and aware and having others care for them for a time, as they slowly rebuild their shattered self.

Being a caretaker is the karma that others choose, in having to take care of people who are handicapped or retarded. The *soul* is never retarded or handicapped. There are many people who seem to be all right physically, yet they're more mentally challenged than anyone.

A person who picks a hard life and who suffers prejudice is far more advanced than one who comes into a situation where society's bias works in their favor. If you look at history, you will see that prejudices such as ethnicity will periodically reverse regarding who is on the top or bottom. So if you're prejudiced and dislike Indians, Asians, blacks, or whites, be very careful, because you're likely to become what you hate. Everyone takes that choice to be of all the races, sexes, sexualities, and body shapes, as well as different stages of wealth or poverty, to see how they'll handle it.

Francine: Let's talk about physical beauty. There are two aspects of this "karma." Some people have earned their physical beauty through many lives in which the soul glows bright. That person's whole visage and all their mannerisms are beautiful.

Other souls may have picked a beautiful body in order to see how they deal with constant laurels and flowers thrown at their feet. This is a very challenging situation to get into, and a very lonely one. Many of your movie stars can have lonely lives, yet another person who takes no notice about their own appearance can be far more beautiful.

Physical beauty is only skin deep—true beauty comes from the soul and shines outward. In this life, if you have nice features, lovely skin, lovely hair, and all the things that really mean something to your own personal appearance, then try to decide whether you've earned it or you chose it. Either way, you can still perfect your soul. There is no entity in the whole world, or on my side, who was not born with some defect. The defect may not be seen or even noticed by others, but the individual will always know it.

Even the most beautiful people will say after they're told they're attractive, "But I don't like my teeth or nose or eyes." That's part of the perfection. There's a fine line between becoming complacent and satisfied in the evolvement of the soul. There must be some internalization and externalization. Once you've done this, then you're not going to pay that much attention. I don't mean that you're not going to keep yourself well kept. If you don't, it's almost as if you don't care about the house in which your soul resides.

Is obesity karmic or charted?

It may be karmic if you starved to death in your prior life. If your glandular system is off, then you charted that. Otherwise, it's a psychological issue where you're "insulating" yourself from life.

Raheim: Obesity is usually an attempt to insulate yourself from being hurt by cruel words that are thrown at you.

In this "consciousness movement" where people are allowed to be their own saviors, the words that will be flung at you are mighty and harsh and cruel. You won't be thrown into the lion's den, but you *will* be criticized for not being idiotic enough to blindly follow some religion. Do you see how irrational that is? God's spark within you is unique and different from every other spark, so how could you all be the same? Instead of following any religion, it should be that everyone is allowed to believe in their own God, their own savior, and their own path to truth. Then we should come together as a group, sharing in the collective God. There is our protection. Don't you see the rationality of that?

Each spark is different, as are our experiences. This must be. One does not experience God the same way as another. God being intellect, you are the emotional side of God experiencing for the intellect. That makes up the totality of God.

Creation has become very complex as far as religion is concerned. It's very much like Sylvia says: "Jesus brought love, as did all the other messengers." But people cannot be satisfied with that. They seem to want hellfire and damnation. The truth of the matter is that the concept of living life after life is, in many ways, far more appalling than a fiery pit.

There comes a point when a soul feels that graduation is upon them because there's no reason to continue. When all the data has been amassed, then you're complete. Does another evolution start? Possibly, but it will not be like this one. It will be on a higher, more intellectual level of learning and expanding on the Other Side or in another universe, if the soul so chooses.

It's no different from saying, "You only have to finish high school, but do you want to go further?" Some will raise their hand and say, "Yes, I want a Ph.D." But those who don't are certainly not looked down upon or thought to be inferior. We are each individuals.

Most people don't like to feel that they're personally responsible for their own devices of forming their own temple and their own salvation. It's much easier, as has been said, to give up your will to another. "Let them write the rules, tell me what I should do, enforce the commandments, and then I don't have to think." Except all of this is unrealistic, because no set of rules ever applies to everyone.

"Thou shalt not kill." But what if someone was about to kill your child? What would any parent do?

"Thou shalt not steal." What if your family was starving?

So you see what I'm getting at? Certainly there's a universal law, but it must primarily be about humanity and caring, concerned with right action. But having too many strict rules guarantees immoral acts. If there's sanction to live freely, there are fewer immoral acts. Pornography, for example, becomes less enticing.

People have always loved "sin." They've always wanted to either participate or watch—the same way in which we're drawn to a horrible accident. But allowing people to be themselves could change that. I don't mean sanctioning criminals, abusers, or psychopaths. We're not talking about that; those are wild, renegade souls who must eventually answer to God. But to constrict and confine human behavior and not let them realize that they're sparks of the Divine, leaving their salvation up to another person—they get nothing but childlike rebellion.

A woman who's been beaten half to death with three children is supposed to stay with a husband because divorce is not allowed? This is not acceptable—it's insane and immoral. That's why society turned to drugs and drinking and violence—because of the strict rules and condemnation, creating a defacement of human dignity.

Francine: Very few entities, regardless of what you may think, really do cruel acts unless they're in a state of derangement. Our basic soul nature is mostly to be good, or seek the good. People may come back due to atrocities they've committed, to experience something of like quality, to see the other side of the coin, but such retributive karma is rare. Most white-souled entities do not have malicious intent to deliberately hurt another. Having guilt, which is sociologically and culturally and religiously impinged upon us, is so wrong. If your motive is pure, you need have no guilt.

Raheim: Don't stay in any situation that's blocking you from being who you are. You may feel that you don't know who you are. That's because you've been split up between your job, your friends, your family, and what everyone else wants you to be and has con-structed you to be.

No parent should put up with ungrateful children, and vice versa. That doesn't mean we want everyone to abandon their families, but there are ways of tolerating situations without being victimized by them.

When your temple gets constructed, nothing can split it. Jesus said, "You may destroy my temple, but it will be rebuilt in three days." Oh, cracks will appear in your essence when you're hurt, but you'll receive Divine glue to smooth it out.

What are the components of synergism?

You must not only *know* that it's possible, but *visualize* that it is. Get two or more together to believe that it has already happened. If you and a friend each have $25, but in your mind you really believe that there will eventually be $50 million, then put it together and think about it as though it were already here. It becomes a reality. Of course, I don't mean gambling.

How can 25 plus 25 become not 50, but 50 million? Synergism means that when you send out your belief into the universe, so to speak, then the universe will move to fulfill your wishes. Energy cre-ates. Have you ever *thought* yourself into a style of dress, hairdo, whatever, and you made it happen? You have synergistically done something to yourself. How did it happen?

That is how Edison did what he did. That is how entrepreneurs do what they do. From nothing, they create everything.

That's making thoughts into things?

Yes. Not only *faith,* but *knowing* that it's real. Physicists still don't understand why, out of a small group of people or ideas, a quantum leap is made that becomes more than the sum of its parts. How does one woman create a church that will eventually have millions of people? Because there is a thought, a belief, a moving together. It is doubled, quadrupled, and so on.

Does the Other Side assist?

Oh, yes, it's not only your program. We see it on the Other Side, we will aid you, and take it into other realms and help it come about. That's why I say that dedication is what pays off. Dedication, belief, and conviction make your thoughts become things. We help you then.

As long as you stay on the road, even if you don't know where you're going, we still see you. The power is truly within the mind. Everyone is a part of God. Everyone is a creative force. You can create in your own realm, in your own world. If that were not the case, there would not have been a Henry Ford, a Thomas Edison. It was not just the fact that they had more infusion, because there are many geniuses walking around who have never done anything with it. They had the belief, brought other people into their belief, and showed them that it was truth. And, as Francine stresses, they would not quit.

Now, the opposite side of this polarity is seen as cults that spring up. There can be a wrong belief. What happens is that people are caught in these psychotic episodes of following one singular person, and they stop using their own intellect to see truth.

How can we become more aware?

You begin by taking parts of yourself and saying, "This day, this week, this month, I'm going to work on noticing and loving plants." It sounds very simplistic, but it's not. You then move on to other parts of your world.

"This day, this week, this month, I'm going to share my essence with an animal. Next, I will try to share feelings with another person. I'm even going to try to be Pantheistic, and I'll sense and feel living spirits in the walls of this room, the washing machine, the tree in the front yard." That extends your antennae.

Years ago, Sylvia used to tell her children, "When something is very good, close your eyes and save it." Do it both ways: When it's very bad, close your eyes and get rid of it instantly. Don't say, "I'll wait until I get home and then I'll deal with this." Too many people do that; by that time, you're infected. You would not wait for hours to wash your hands if you had plague-causing germs on them.

You can visualize somebody being free of addictions. They may not get out of the drug mode at that particular time, but if there are enough of you visualizing that person healthy, it will happen. However, the more "good" rises up, here or wherever the consciousness movement is rising, the more negativity will rise along with it. It's a battle. Some people can be manipulated by the dark side of things—I don't mean a "devil," but I'm talking about negativity that rises up, and a person who is susceptible at the time will react on it. That's where they got the idea of "demon possession." It's not.

A person who is off-track becomes vulnerable to negativity. Or, if they're drug infected, they become an open door to all the negativity in a room, in the world, in the traffic, and they'll react. They may even strike out at the very person who has done them the most good, because some people don't want to be healed.

Now, let's go further with that. Let's say you visualize a person whole and healed, but this doesn't seem to work. Let me tell you something mysterious that happens: Your intended person may not get it, but someone else will benefit. It's never wasted.

That healthy being you constructed will fit the next person who comes along in need of it. Haven't you ever heard someone say, "I don't know why, but I was into alcohol (or drugs or smoking, whatever), and all of a sudden, one day I just gave it up"? Somewhere, a group was programming.

It's the same as love. Everyone cries, "I love so-and-so, but they don't love me back." Love goes out and another person catches it. Realize that all this is transient. It all passes away. I cannot stress that enough. Indeed, life is precious and children are wonderful, as are plants and animals, but you're only here for a short visit.

The way to avoid manipulation by the world's negativity is to realize that this life is not the end-all and be-all. There are other lives to be lived, for some, and certainly the Other Side awaits. How excited can you get about being at camp for a week? That's all that life is. But, my God, you're proud of yourself when you've gone through it.

There is not one soul, regardless of what you think of them, who is not proud of themselves when they cross over. At least they went through it. They might not have passed all tests gracefully, but they're proud that they even had the courage to come down.

Is expanding our aura a protection?

Spread your aura. Think of your aura as going out 30 feet or more; you can make it go that far. When you come into a room, think of your aura expanding and breathing as a living thing. Your aura is a real electrical emanation around you, the same as the saints were painted with halos. Think of it expanding and bathing the whole room in your light.

Anyone who wants to minister to others can do so. There is no doubt about that. You are right on the brink of breaking through, as Francine says, to the greatest epiphany that you'll ever see. She refers to the rebirth of religious belief as it should be. Organized religion should never have been organized, because then it became big business. That's frightening.

God is everywhere?

God is ever-present in your everyday lives, not just in a church. The only reason for people to share a common knowledge is to work in a different area for God, then to understand that individualistic area and work toward acceptance of those differences. You are of one God with many minds. A slow learner is just as good as the honor roll student, because all types are needed to make up a classroom.

Can guides see negativity in a room?

When a room is filled with positive energy, it's a bright, golden-tinged, rose light. When it's filled with negativity, it looks like cheesecloth—hazy and "swampwater green." It has a texture and a stickyness to it. Every one of you has been in a situation in which you felt the air "thicken" around you. Or you felt that you couldn't breathe, the atmosphere was heavy, or the energy felt morbid and stifling. It had nothing to do with whether the room was hot.

In this type of situation, please be aware of your solar plexus. Whenever you're in a negative atmosphere, you might start getting sick to your stomach, even when you don't have the flu. Similarly, you might get a headache right away even though you have no sinus problems, because your body will biologically react to the negative energy.

Should we confront negative situations?

Yes, but in human form, most of you are terrified to do that. You see, negativity can become a security; like the way in which any job or particular role becomes secure the more we do it. Then we get ourselves knee-deep in the mire, and we can't get out. I don't advise you throwing caution to the wind, because you have to eat and sleep. There's nothing wrong with wanting material gain—a car that runs, clothes that look nice, and, for God's sake, food that's tasty. God didn't mean that only a select few would have plenty. That's ridiculous.

There's nothing more disgusting than someone not clean and

wearing sackcloth and ashes outside, asking for alms. Our Lord never did that, and neither did any other avatars. Buddha was a prince from a wealthy family. Even though he *did* walk the streets of the people, he had old money following him that took care of his every need. Jesus also came from a very wealthy family. It's only logical. He was from the House of David. He was from royalty.

When Our Lord said, "Give it all up and follow me," he did not mean to drop all worldly goods, but rather, religious bigotries. No one was more committed than the Magdalene; she was the most dedicated. She was not necessarily an apostle, but she was certainly a disciple.

Are there both universal and individual truths?

Absolute truth is perfect and unbounded. There's also individual truth, which applies solely to you. Some of the many universal truths include the following:

- Each individual must seek after their own salvation.
- Do not harm another human being, but you must have righteous anger against wrongdoing.
- Accept no guilt for your actions if your motive is pure.
- Judge not.

If you devise a personal truth that is in conflict with a universal truth, then you're in error. It means you've "disconnected" from God.

Can wrongs be justified from your side?

Let's say a mother wants her home divided between two daughters after her death, but one daughter uproots the will, forges it, and takes everything against the mother's wishes. The mother can then, because this discomfort follows her to the Other Side, create a situation or "manipulation" where there will be a retributive act down the road.

You know the old adage, "They may gain it, but they will not be happy with it"? It's true.

I've heard that we should open our minds to infusion because we only use 4 or 5 percent of our brains.

Yes, you're absolutely right. Once you open up, you're working with 90 percent or more of the brain. You've been told it can't be so, but trust me, it's analogous to when no one knew the world was round. This is very much like the brain. That little section is all that's used.

But if someone told you that you could use more, then you wouldn't have to be controlled and confined. You can explore so many other regions. I take issue that there's so much money spent on exploring outer space, when the mind is the most wondrous, unfathomable space. Between your ears is where humankind's journey should be. The mind is illuminating, awe-inspiring, and God connecting.

But you're fighting 500,000 years of genetic, religious, and sociological programming. When you come back to the Other Side, you know that if you incarnate again, you're going to be a little smarter. Then in the next life, you're a little better, but the old shell fits too tightly. When we come into human form, we forget. We get afraid, we get lax, and we take the easiest path.

It's very frightening, although thrilling, to know that you're your own God-center, your own task master, the pilot of your own ship— thrilling and yet scary. But the true captain is God. The only place that you're going to fall is toward Him anyway, regardless of what waters you go through. He's not going to let you sink. You may crash the ship, but your soul will never sink.

Synergism occurs by just knowing?

Realize that your goal is real. You see, Christopher Columbus knew something was there when he sailed west to find India. Synergism is created by the belief that it is possible, in the knowledge that it will be; then you act upon it.

It sounds so simple. "I believe I'm a psychic, a prophet. I believe that I report directly from God, that my channel is open. I shall act upon it regardless of how silly or ridiculous or self-effacing it may be at first. I will do it." Then it multiplies. That is what synergism is: truly becoming what you act upon or believe you are.

Every person perceives reality differently. Everything is you. It's all in your reality. If you're treated badly, it's because you've allowed it. If you're treated well, it's because you've demanded it. If you have a good job, you worked for it. If you don't have a good job, you should move on. It's as simple as that. Don't walk around in "sackcloth and ashes," crying that the world is against you—because it's not! *You* are against you. *You* are self-defeating.

You make your own world, and you must live within it or change it for the better.

How It Works

Francine: Synergism is the act of taking a small grain of your goal, then expanding on it to create the whole.

Let me explain. Let's say you're trying to procure money that's rightfully yours. Take a dollar, and concentrate on the dollar to make it grow. Concentrate on the fact that this dollar reproduces itself many times, a million times if you want—don't be afraid. Take that dollar and give it to another person. But make sure that this person is also someone in need. You don't want someone to make a habit out of panhandling on the street, because that's not helping them. That's what synergism means.

You've enacted for the universe what you want. You've put your needs or your wants into motion and started a chain reaction. You also must give conditions to it: "When this grows, I will get so much. I will then give so much to someone else helping the needy, the poor, the homeless." That's what tithing really meant. It was not intended to make the church rich. It was meant to go into the gigantic pot, from which everybody could be taken care of.

To help affirm your goal as real, devise a visual aid. If you want to be thin, get something that is imitative of that, a thin body picture. Then cut out a picture of your face, and put it on that thin body. Begin to program your mind by projecting yourself onto the slimness of that body. Put it someplace where you can view it at all times.

What is also nice to do is to get a very large bulletin board or tack board. Place your goals on that board so you see it often. You can pin up a dollar bill, a picture of a person whom you want to look like, or a car or house you want—all the "wish" things, your synergistic things.

You may say to me, "What if I was never meant to have $2 million?" Then you would not get it, but another will. That's how synergism works. Let's say you want your heart to be better: Find a biology book with a heart picture; put it up on your tack board; and ask for a vibrant, beating, healthy heart. It would be also be good to put a picture of a body up with the whole circulatory system. Begin to program your mind that this is your body, with healthy blood coursing through it. The more senses you can appeal to, the more effective this process becomes. To program for money, immerse yourself in its color, feel, and aroma.

Just make a contractual agreement, "When I get this, I promise to give so much to good, to charity, to the homeless, etc." You don't want to win just for yourself. If you do, the synergism dies. There's nothing wrong with saying, "I want this to take care of my family. That's okay, too. Just include anybody you want along with yourself. "I will give 40 percent to my family, or whatever amount." You must make it a contractual agreement, and program for that.

With whom do I make this contract?

God, the ultimate Contractor. Connect to the Divine resource. People need to know that all of their thoughts swirl in the atmosphere. It depends on who will connect to it, and who will be tenacious enough to pull it down into action. That's why some people are "lucky" and some are not. They don't know how to attach their life to that giant umbilical cord from God. They don't realize they can be fed.

Another example of synergy is an architect who goes into the middle of the field holding in her hand two bricks. She looks at the field and says, "From these two bricks, I will build a shopping center." And what happens? From those two bricks come in other bricks and work-ers. The synergistic dream is built. If a person can do that with two bricks or two million bricks, you can also do that with your life.

Sylvia: Unlike a lot of channels, I do not believe that you *totally* create your own reality. I know that is a popular theme now, but the problem I have is, what happens if your reality is not at all like my reality? I think it makes a person just too powerful.

We create our own environment, our own positive or negative reality. In that way, we are the creative force of God. If you believe in something long enough and can make it real in your mind, it will happen. Francine told me years ago, "The only reason that things do not happen, or that people do not get their wishes fulfilled, is because they 'cash in their chips' too early. They give up."

It helps if you're willing to believe in something greater than your-self. It does not have to be overly altruistic. It does not have to change the world. It can be as minimal as having a happy family, a love affair, or enough money. In doing that, really visualize it and program for it.

People have said to me, "Is it wrong to want material things?" No. However, if your sole focus is on material things, then that's wrong. But while we're camping out on Earth, there is nothing wrong with having a nice bunk and a clean floor. Rather than stay-ing in a rat-infested hole, we're perfectly right in asking for nice accommodations.

I think in this life, as we spiritually advance, we truly know that the power of God, the God Consciousness, and Mother God's spirit moves through us. We carry the genes of not only our Earthly parents, but also our Divine parents. We can be much more powerful than we realize.

Church is important, for by coming together, we exude power. Religion was really meant to be for mutual support of like-minded people. We were meant to help each other along the journey of life, and to add our energy and synergism to another's.

HEALING MEDITATION

I want you to ask that you, and every single person in your life, begin to receive healing energy from Mother God, Father God, the God Consciousness, and the Holy Spirit. The intellectual and emotional sides of yourself are now open like a channel to God.

Feel every organ and every system in your body moving toward its optimal mode of performance, without causing any stress to you. Rule out every unnecessary pain, especially mental pain, the worries about finances, children, husbands, wives, parents. Let it all go. Give it to God.

I want you to see a road in front of you. The road appears smooth, and on either side are beautiful trees, birds, and flowers. It really is the road of your life, symbolically. I want you to stand there. Before you take your first step forward from this point, demand that the road smooth out, filling all gullies or cracks, and removing all rejections or disappointments ahead of you.

If, by chance something is hidden there, you will sail through it. You will be able to go very fast and catch the breeze. Feel your lungs fill with pure air and your eyesight getting better. Every sense is functioning perfectly. You feel more alive than ever before, and a certainty of strength comes from Almighty God.

Remember that this earth is only a transient place. Things are just things. But at the end of that road, you are going to cross a beautiful stream and go to the Other Side. There, you'll meet all the loved ones you have known in every life, as well as this one. You'll feel, as I have felt, how foolish we can be sometimes laboring over one little crack in the road when, if you just speed a little faster, you get past it.

You may say, in your heart of hearts, "But I'm tired." I know you are, but run anyway. Run a little faster. Push yourself a little more, and you'll get past the negative. Ask for blessings. Demand them from God. God is not concerned if you make demands. You are demanding of your own God-center as well.

Demand that your loved ones begin to be healed, that everyone stabilizes, that there is no darkness or negativity around anyone, that the place where you work brightens up, and that where you live shines with God's light.

Let go of all those useless, guilty feelings: "I did not do; I should do; I wish I had done." You would not have done them anyway, and most likely you shouldn't have. If you got divorced, if someone left you, if you moved, don't feel regret. Those were not mistakes; that was your charted road. We can't stay still; we must move on. Feel God's forgiveness now, and the lack of guilt that resides in your heart.

A Prayer

Dear God,

We are strong, fearless, faithful, continuous, and loyal. We may have many human failings to overcome, because we live in a human body, but nevertheless, our soul will shine through it all. Our hearts mean well. Our minds mean right. Any mental, physical, or spiritual illness that is in my body, let it be rinsed out and removed. I feel your energy surging through. I will live with dignity. When it comes time for us to die, we will die easily with dignity.

On My Side

Raheim: Let me explain a little bit about what we do on the Other Side—my side. We are able to construct things by thought; by thought alone, we can make something happen; by thought alone, we create reality. Everyone has this ability, but tragically, it is lost in the descent into life.

For many years, Francine has told you that you don't realize the power you have and can call on. It's because you're fighting against an imaginary gravitational pull—the reality that's been constructed for you by culture, society, and religion. So you're caught in the web of what you believe, which limits your lateral moves as far as what you can do.

I'm not saying you can levitate yourself—you can't. You could, possibly, if you spent years and years trying to demagnetize yourself. But what a loss to your spirituality by spending 30 years just to float two feet off the ground. It seems like a great waste of energy to me.

Synergism is a far more useful phenomenon that we live on, on my side. Jesus was such a teacher, such a metaphysician, such a psychic. He taught us to gather together two or more in his name. The Bible has not expounded on this in its totality. You can use any name that is sacred and powerful to you, not just Jesus'. In this way, you can create a synergistic reality. Gnostics, for instance, are brought together synergistically by the common bond of their belief. A few decades ago, there was no such thing as Novus Spiritus. But in the mind of one person, it was a reality. That reality was made into a concrete phenomenon. When it became a reality, what happened? People came.

With Sylvia, people began to synergistically form a religious body of thought, which began to move forward in an ancient process and became a renewed religion that is now growing with great fervor. Even though you do not see the numbers, they multiply across the country. People are hearing about study groups every day.

Now consider the same process on a smaller scale. In your own lives, make your own reality. Doubt is the one thing you have to fight. The important question is: What exactly do you want? Most human beings, in all their wonderful personas and flavors, want nebulous things. "I want money," they say. Or power, fame, health, beauty, or a loved one or a child.

When people do not get exactly what they want in the form they expect, they don't know how to redirect that synergism and transfer it to another area. Let's say that you're a woman who wishes to have a child, but because of your chart, you're barren. Now, you can synergistically program for a natural child until you die, and it will never be a possibility. All that energy goes into that one aspect that will never be. If it will never be, take all that energy and put it into, let's say, adopting children, taking care of children, doing good works for children.

People have a set notion of what they synergistically want. If they don't get it, they give up. But energy is energy. It can be converted into something else just as magnificent. Those who are most successful take from one area and put it on another track so that it runs. In running that new track, they become successful.

Perhaps you're saying to yourself, "But I want a man (or woman), and I have not gotten one. Why not? Wasn't it preordained that I should get it?" The problem is that timing can be delayed. Instead of waiting around feeling self-pity and wondering *why,* you should make yourself go out, be a part of life, and do good deeds and good actions. Don't put all your energy onto one path.

In transferring the energy, doors will open. The negative block was, "I didn't get it. I want it; where is it?" You see, maybe your lesson was to learn to redirect your mind toward something else before your goal is realized. The old adage is, "The horse comes galloping when you least expect it." And like the ancient adage, "It is very hard to wait for someone who comes not." Well, then, wait only until someone else comes. And in the meantime, while you're waiting for the special one to come, love those around you. Now you've put into perspective what spirituality truly means.

On the Other Side, when we want to construct something, several people get together and we begin to focus our thoughts. We've built coliseums and marvelous edifices. If we don't like the way a certain column is, we tear it down with our mind and rebuild it until our collective vision is achieved.

You say, "That's fantastic." No, it's no fantasy. All the buildings and things in your world were first constructed in someone's mind. That mind is the one that put it into being. The minute the mind has constructed it, it's there. Mortar, glass, tile, beams—those are only the physical aspects.

You'd be surprised that your Gnostic temple stands on my Side.

It makes every temple that you've ever seen look paltry. It has a rounded dome. It looks like Saturn with a spiral going around the side, with slanted blue glass that lets rose-colored light through. There's no reason you cannot synergistically put it together in your world.

Who do you want in your life? What does this person look like? How do you make meeting him or her happen? Now, you can't sit in your house and program for that and expect someone to walk up to the door. You can't hope that they'll knock on your car window and say, "Here I am." But it *does* come true. We know that thoughts are things, because we see your thoughts becoming things. And unfortunately, some are pretty horrifying—especially what you sometimes think of yourself. One guide told me that his loved one was thinking about what she would look like when she became very old. He said to me, "The grotesqueness of what she thought of herself and how she might look was horrifying."

Why not program yourself to look elegant in your elder years, with grace, rather than gnarled and shriveled with a forgetful memory. You do not realize the power of your mind to create what you'd like it to. I don't want you to get paranoid that every time you have a phobia or speak of fearful things that you'll create them. No, fears have nothing to do with programming. Those are usually morphic resonances from a past life.

Can negative thoughts alter your chart?

They can't alter it, but they can clog or delay it and make it thick. Conversely, positive thoughts can make everything speed up. Think of a negative thought as a tree lying in the middle of a road. Now, the road is still there, and eventually somebody will lift the tree off, but you can have a great big tree right over your soul's highway.

It's very difficult to remain positive in a negative world. If you *do* manage it, then others will show you the horrors; if you try to be positive, others will try to program you to be tired, sick, lonely, old, destitute, or whatever the case might be.

Every time you say, "I didn't get what I wanted to have; why not?" you're moving backward. Only *you* can prevent that. You'll get fulfilled if you stop negatively programming. For as great as synergism builds, negativity tears. So, unfortunately, in the human self, you're always fighting yourself—you're building, you're tearing; you're building, you're tearing.

I'm not so far removed from life that I don't remember how terribly difficult it is to keep positive, because negative is easier. The negative, in a way, is a comfort zone. Negativity is free from surprise; however, it is also free from joy and emotion. In misery and depression, you don't have to get up, wash yourself, brush your hair, or move around. You sink into it and wallow in it.

Most people understand it when you say, "I'm in a bad mood. I'm depressed. I'm beaten." But on the other hand, people don't understand when you say, "I'm in such a good mood. I'm joyous and happy." They say, "What's this? What's happening?" It's human.

Sylvia uttered one of her many marvelous pearls today. She gives them out as droplets. Today she said, "Insecurity builds, ego destroys." We thought about that for a long time, and then we saw how true it is.

Insecurity has always been defined as a negative emotion, yet it can be a motor, a driving force. "I'm insecure, but I'm going to work harder to be better." Ego says, "I've already arrived. I'm perfectly satisfied."

The false ego believes that it's always right and doesn't need to change, but an insecure person is always striving for perfection. To survive and to strive for excellence is the highest form of spirituality and synergism.

No human being is always right—not in human form, unless they're acting under Divine right actions. You can't even say that attaining the love of another human being, which is higher than yourself, is always right. But you can be sure that with pure motive, you can't be wrong.

"I'm perfect; I'm elevated; I'm supreme; I've earned the right to be happy." This last phrase is the one we find to be the most hysterical—you have earned *nothing* in life. You can't. You only get rewards on the Other Side. You chalk up points, but you don't get the benefits until later. How can you earn something you made a contract for?

That's not what spirituality means. People constantly say, "That person had such a horrible life. Wouldn't it have been great if they could have been rewarded?" Not here in this "boot camp."

In the action of living is where your wealth is generated. In the deepest trenches of life's struggles is where spiritual wealth comes from. We hear so many people's prayers, if they're not silenced to us. All of us want to say to all of you, "Stop." You should only pray for things that are possible, not impossible.

If you are 5'2", don't pray to be 5'9". It won't happen. Now, you *could* spend your whole life wishing you were taller, putting all your energy into that wish. Instead, put that energy to good use. The vehicle that you're wearing is not that important; just keep yourself healthy.

If I said to you, "You have a long trip to take; I want you to go in a broken-down car," you would say to me, "Oh, no. I might not go all the way." Yet, you drive your broken-down bodies all over, and you don't care. You run out of gas; you don't have the right fuel; people steal your hubcaps; you have no tread on your tires. You run it at high speed, and pray, "Please, can I have more protection?" And we send archetypes in to coat your tires, to fix everything that we can to keep the motor going, and you still run it too fast. You put all manner of bad things in your mouth and pray every night that we'll protect you. You then get mad at God if He and She do not—and you feel that you've been abandoned. You wonder why Mr. or Ms. Right does not come along. When hasn't it ever dawned on you that *you* may not be Mr. or Ms. Right yourself?

"I don't have any friends." Are *you* one?

"I'm not loved." Do *you* love?

"I don't get anything." Do *you* give?

"I'm never forgiven." Do *you* forgive?

These are the oldest lessons in the world, and each time we come in as babies, we must learn the same old lessons. We have to be fed, nurtured, and taken care of—except we never really get over that. We *still* need to be nurtured and cared for and held. Never once do we think to hold, feed, or nurture *ourselves*.

Synergism can be very metaphysical or very scientific. True synergism is, "I will create." Then gather more people to create with you—a body of health, a body of movement, a body of belief, a purpose higher than yourself. Whatever you wish to accomplish in order to be a higher, more spiritual being.

Now, you notice I haven't talked about monetary wealth. The wealth of the soul is all I'm concerned with. You don't have to wear rags, but it's far better to have your spirit soar than to be dressed in finery and be bankrupt in spirit. You're not going to take your finery with you to the Other Side. You'll be stripped of all those external trappings that seem to identify you.

In each life, do not diminish your soul—elevate it. Grow. Grow your soul larger. Those are your riches. All the little things that you worry about—don't let them grow into big monsters. Synergism works both ways. Things grow into monstrosities of phobic reaction and fear—or into beauty, belief, and comfort. You must discern, and be a sieve. Some information is kept; some pours out.

Can we actually destroy negativity?

Absolutely. You can dissipate it and make it go away. You can do it individually, but it is so much easier as a group of even two or three. You have no idea what you can do, synergistically, in a strong group.

Do churches encourage group synergism?

Absolutely. That's the only reason why churches have any benefit. You're perfectly within your right to all ask for individual things. You're there for one common purpose—to get better. Gnostics have always had the insight to know that people gather together for a common bond, whether it's to worship or to bring peace or love or joy to each other.

Church is *not* for God Almighty.

Coming together creates the power to get you through the week. Whether you realize it or not, the God in each one of you is responding back and forth. It resonates. We can see it build like a pyramid.

A singular person, out there wandering alone, can pray and pray and pray. That's not bad, but this individual does not have the benefit of synergism.

Some people have a chapel in their home where they pray. That's all well and good, but its effectiveness is diminished. Jesus said, "Come together." Buddha said it. Mohammed said it. Appolonius said it. They all knew the power of synergism. Each entity adds more power of God. When you add your God-center to someone else's, their God-center is added to yours. That's what it's about.

Has anybody made a building in bad taste?

Yes. Oh, I have. I made a cement tent once that was frighteningly ugly. It was terrible. I tried to make something totally private. I don't know whether you know this or not, but I do a lot of imitative magic. However, I had no ventilation, and I almost suffocated. You may find this to be amazing, but we breathe; we have organs. They are all on opposite sides from yours. We don't have bodily functions like you do, though.

Why do you have organs on the Other Side?

We've often thought about that. We think it's to create a mirror image of the physical self to ease the shock of incarnating. I think we just carry it over with us. My heart beats. I can breathe.

Familiarity is a powerful force. Come to think of it, I don't know of anyone who doesn't have organs. There may be some whom I've never asked, but I know that almost all of us have hearts that beat.

If you never incarnated, would you still have organs?

Yes. Every time we have seen the visage of Father or Mother God, they have the expected exteriors of the male and female. Of course, the Father cannot hold His form for very long, although Azna does.

What if you suffocate on the Other Side?

Well, I would not die. In my tent, I couldn't breathe and I was terribly uncomfortable. Finally, I became clever enough to realize that I had no ventilation.

Is psychokinesis—moving objects with the mind—a form of synergism?

Oh, absolutely it is. Some humans have that and others do not. Just as some people are psychic, and others are stupid or smart, entities are entities. Not everybody on my side is smart, you know. Not everybody is clever or happy. I don't mean to be negative, but everybody keeps their same personality. Some are dolts.

Wishes

I am very pleased with how you're learning, but there are secrets that you still don't know because you don't yet know the *questions* to ask.

All the wishes that you have go into a safe place. They are "prismed" for safekeeping and are allotted out at given moments. We can disperse answers to your wishes when the time is right. This does not disturb charts, option lines, windows, or emotions that you're working on. But it's a sprinkling, I guess you might say, of *luck,* that is allowable in your dream state. Many of these wishes can only be used *once,* like the windows of opportunity that may never come again if you pass them up. It sounds like the genie's "three wishes" of legend. A specific wish can only be used once with total fervency.

This happens from the very time that you're a child, and sometimes these wishes are bestowed on you in the most inopportune moments. Let's say that when you were two years old you wanted a teddy bear but didn't get one. Now, at age 30, you're dating a man who brings you a teddy bear. The amazing thing is that the reality that was then is *still* in the time of God.

Why get a childhood wish in adulthood?

The wish is dropped on you at random if you don't have the knowledge of *when* to ask for it. In other words, it's very much like wanting a new car really badly and wishing for it. Then with hard work, you buy your new car, but weeks later you *win* a new car. Your wish has come true beyond itself. So, what you must do is say, "*I want it now.*"

A wish doesn't always come at the time it's needed unless you specifically ask for it. That's the reality that we see. Because our timing is off, we have to get synchronized with you. All kinds of treasures belong to you, but you haven't had sense enough to ask for them. We have a trust fund, but nobody to claim it.

You must be specific. Don't just say that you're hungry—say specifically what you want to eat. The same with your dreams. You may ask me, "If I've asked for a perfect mate, does that mean that I got one a long time ago and lost him? Is my window of opportunity closed, never to reopen?" No. If that mate had been perfect, you wouldn't have lost him or her.

You must now start asking for *perfect* health and wealth. Do not be afraid to ask for wealth, but make it significant. Don't just ask for $50,000—that's too short-sighted; it won't take you through a long life.

Be *specific* enough. Say, "I want to have perfect wealth that will keep me in a very comfortable position for as long as I am in this world." Now, your wish for money has become a practical reality. Too often, someone wishes for just enough money to pay for a car, or for some other immediate need.

Why not start putting wishes in your "wish bank"? The angels are the "controllers" of your wishes. That doesn't mean wishes that don't come from God, but they are bestowed by angels. No wish that gets fulfillment is ever selfish.

Don't be afraid to ask for as much as your mind can think of. God wants every entity living on this planet to have a long, happy life. I cannot stress that enough. You don't have to be any more ill than you wish to be, or any heavier or thinner, any poorer or lonelier.

Why are you besieged by illness? Because you were programmed

****

from every direction by medical and sociological stress. You constantly hear warnings based upon your age, by the era you live in, by a certain job, and by the sense that you are alone. You hear statistics on *everything*.

Regardless, your chart is set, and you will *not* die until your time has come. But what about fulfilling the wish to be more well, free from illness? Absolutely. When your wish comes at the same time that your window of opportunity opens, miracles occur. You say, "Well, how do I make that occur?" By *asking* for it.

Say, "My window is *now*, God. I want my wish to descend immediately. But make it so that the window sill, the sash, and everything else is *perfect*. When you ask for health and enough money, ask for it wisely; ask for it to comfortably sustain you. You can even ask for more than you need so that you can help others.

You can do it within a week's time. You can retrieve the wishes that you had from childhood. Let's say a child wanted to be a painter or a priest. Life went by, and the person grew to 40 or 50. The person finally decides to go to college, and graduates at age 60. The wish caught up with the want, and the window opened. Of course, it's the angels that handle wishes.

The reality that you want on Earth exists in my world of other dimensions. If you don't live your dreams, you haven't withdrawn your trust that you built up in life. Don't use your wishes frivolously. In other words, when you wish for health, don't say, "I want my son or my daughter to be well today. No. Say, *"For their entire lives."*

Prayer is a confirmation that a hope or a wish will be granted, that the opportunity will appear. What if you wish and nothing happens? If you keep wishing, using prayer with specifics attached, it will come about. Activation is also very important—the activation that you're worth more mentally and physically. If you act the part, you *become* it.

It doesn't mean ego. But rather than walk around shabbily, dress the best that you can. Act proud, full of mirth and health. If you *act* well, you will *be* well.

Have glory in the strength of yourself, in the beauty of your soul.

How can I strip away the facades of my life?

When facades are taken away, souls speak to each other. There are very few times in life when people can strip away their facades and let someone see them naked. I think that this is one of the things that Sylvia has in her favor. She safely allows a person to reveal themselves completely to her. They feel no judgment, and they are able to cleanse. That is the way I want all of you to be.

Be able to reach toward people. Say, "God, make it so that each soul who approaches me does so honestly. Let me hear the soul's cry—the *honesty* of the soul." Now, be willing to take the consequences for this, because when that wish drops, you may find yourself being faced with some very vicious people, who you thought were your friends. When that facade drops, it is almost like seeing with x-ray eyes some things that will surprise you.

Say, "God, let me perceive people as they really are. My wish is to see the soul's cry, the internal workings of the soul." You may find that suddenly you don't like the person you're married to or the person you've been with. Then, maybe you start liking a person whom you thought you didn't like before.

You may also state during this time: "I would like my energy to be transmitted to every other human being, and in turn, their energy will be transmitted to me." This is the closest you will ever get on your side to merging. It is a wonderful, uplifting thing to want to touch the soul of another human being and share part of their essence.

Does touching a soul help with healing?

You will be able to see the darkness in the soul, and back away, or you will be able to see the beauty in the soul. You will no longer have to worry about whether a soul is dark or light. If you keep the mirrors and the light around you, you can still touch but *not absorb*. I'm not worried about you getting too close and absorbing the dark, because that really signals itself nowadays. You don't have to worry about these aspects being hidden. Their "horns" come right up within five minutes. It used to be more insidious.

What did Jesus mean when he said, "The Father and I are one"?

The will of God is the same as *your* will. People don't realize that. Keep asking for that knowledge. Too often, people give up their will to others. As Sylvia says, they begin to live through the will of someone else. But if you really listen inside yourself, you'll find that the pure will of God and yourself become one and the same. It really means, humbly and pridefully, that you become a *tool* that God uses.

When you release your will to God, you becomes a shooting star, a beacon of light, a candle in the darkness. People are so afraid to give up their will to God for fear they will be crucified in some way. But in fact, the only true happiness comes when God steers your ship.

God's will does not force you into a life of deprivation. In fact, all things come then. Even if things are taken from you, it doesn't matter because your soul is so happy that external things are unnecessary.

What is the value of doing past-life regressions?

One of the main benefits of doing hypnotic regression is that it can bring forward the tremendous knowledge and talents that we have garnered in past lives. Regression is a wonderful tool to get rid of phobias, but what is sadly neglected is that so many beautiful things can be brought forward, such as artistic or medical skills. Also, you can purge any leftover "spiritual garbage" and bring your guides in with authentic truth.

I work at a religious school, but I feel so stifled because of the dogma.

Yes, but you are becoming a beacon of light within that dogma. You are probably the *only* shaft of light they have—in your non-denominational beauty, in your love. That is probably the only fresh air they have in that stuffy place. Do not let them control your head. Gnostics, during the great upheaval when the "Christian" church was trying to get a foothold, were called heretics and evil priests because they kept speaking the truth.

Gnostics said, "There is a Mother and a Father God, for whom we must seek our own understanding. We are *not* going to be control people. We will not let somebody else speak for us, or be filled with dogma and irrational depictions of God."

And for that they were burned.

What are Akashic Records?

They are the infinitely vast repository of all events for all time. You could think of them as God's memory. They are an actual *living* thing. When you are on the Other Side and you want to revisit and experience something, you can go into the Akashic Records and relive it in full essence and experience. When you are on the Other Side, your full essence is present with you, not split into pieces for each Earth life.

Will people view Sylvia's life?

Yes. She doesn't care. Anything you ask her about her life, she will tell you. She's the most open person in the world. She hides nothing. Some people are more secretive; they don't want their lives to be open. But I don't think there is any part of Sylvia's life that she would hide. She is intruded upon all the time.

§ Chapter Five §

Tenets for Living

Sylvia: The tenets are the foundation of our whole religious belief. Our church, Novus Spiritus, is built on them. When you read these tenets, they may seem to be too forgiving and quite loosely hung together, but I want you to understand that they are *literal meanings*.

These words give me such great comfort. When I am in dire straits, I read through them and they ease my soul. Francine gave us these tenets many years ago.

Tenet 1
The way of all peace is to scale the mountain of Self. The love of others makes the climb down easier. We see all things darkly until love lights the lamp of the soul.

Now, you may think that this is just a pretty poem. But people are always saying to me, "Sylvia, how do I find peace of mind? How do I find true inner happiness?" The only way you can do so is to *get out of yourself*. If you get too "body bound" and too much into yourself, you're going to become closed off, morose, unhappy, depressed, down, and ill. We were never supposed to inhabit this body totally.

This body is what a car is to a person. Are we the car? No. We are the driver of that vehicle. We utilize the car to enact our lives. However, there is a fine line—keep yourself a little bit "in" and a little bit "out." How do you do this? Think of yourself about four inches away from your body. Ask God each night to keep you there.

You know that if you're alone too much and you sit around and think too much, you get very depressed. But let a friend call you from outside—you get all excited, because the caller has broken through the barrier of yourself. Turning your focus to the caller, you are now loving them, and not so concerned with your aches and pains, or whether your kids love you, or what happened to your marriage. You moved outside of yourself.

Everything, eventually, takes care of itself anyway, whether you like it or not. Most things, left alone, will work themselves out one way or the other. Don't get me wrong: We must still directly confront some things that face us. We have to confront the evilness that comes to us in life. But most of the time, this is not the case. Like the great philosopher says, and I have quoted this to so many of my clients, "When in doubt, do nothing."

A lot of times, life itself will move *you* along. Somebody said to me the other day, "Sylvia, maybe it's not right that I come to you. Maybe I should live my own chart."

I said, "Yes, but there's nothing wrong with stopping at a gas station when you're lost and asking for directions, is there?" I think that's what we are when we're ministering to people. We are "gas stations" for people who get lost and can't read the map. It's no wonder that men appear at a psychic's door less frequently than women. Men don't want to ask for directions.

Tenet 2
Whatever thou lovest, lovest thou.

That's true. You say, "No, no, Sylvia, I loved someone who didn't love me." What you don't understand is that when you give love out and it doesn't come back to you through that person, it will come back through someone else. Also, when your love isn't reflected, then your chart has intervened.

We are so stupid, all of us. Somebody on the left is barking, "I love you. I love you. I love you." And we say, "Yeah, I know, but I'm only looking straight ahead."

Love comes back. It becomes a swirling, magnificent, marvelous volcano that erupts and pours on you. It would be like if everything in my life fell apart and I said, "I don't have any love in my life," then looking out and knowing that some of you love me, as I love you. How stupid of me not to know that.

The Gnostic movement is the beating heart of love. You've got to be able to approach that beating heart. If we have any strength at all, it's that. People come to my church, they tell me, to be rejuvenated and to "plug in." That's what we want. Come in and plug into us. Get filled up. Get your love. Then go out and whip the world with one hand tied behind your back. Don't be so concerned about having Mr. or Ms. Right. There are many of them out there to choose from. We always think that because we don't have a warm body next to us all the time, we're not loved.

We shoot through life like a falling star. That is all we are. Just one little star in the heavens that swiftly crosses. And while we streak across, we ought to create some friction in the stratosphere to make light—and to do that we have to love.

I love it when people ask, "Who can I love?" I always want to say, "Look around you. Reach out to the person next to you." I have actually been with strangers in a place, and reached over and grabbed somebody's hand. I have never once, ever, had anybody turn their hand away from me.

You say, "Well, I feel embarrassed." Why? What is the worst—rejection? Big deal, we get that all the time—just move on.

Tenet 3

*Do not give unto God any human pettiness such as
vengeance, wrath, or hate. Negativity is man's alone.*

I love the third tenet. It is so wonderful, slashing deeply into the
dogma of any religion that would deny it. Do not put petty, silly, jeal-
ous things unto God. That diminishes the supreme, omnipotent, all-
loving, perfect Entity. He is never interested in vengeance or negativity. I am constantly amazed that people don't think about what it
means to say that God is all-loving.

Think. Think. When you read the Bible or any text, think. Why
would God be vengeful toward the Ammonites? Didn't He make them
as well as the Samaritans, the Pharisees, and the Sanhedrin? Of course
He did. God was supposed to have gotten mad at the Ammonites, so
He killed thousands of them? Wrong. Don't put that kind of
vengeance on God. *Do not* think that God plays favorites.

When we rise up to meet God, we become like children, because
we choose God. That is really what the term *chosen people* meant.
They chose God.

PURIFYING MEDITATION

*Put your hands upward on your thighs. Ask for all the
archetypes, the prophets, the saints, Mother and Father God,
our guides, Jesus, and the love of the Holy Spirit to descend on
us today and pull out the root of fear, even if it is a seedling.
The weeds keep multiplying in our garden, which is our mind
ruled by fear. Rip them out and call them by name. The ill-
nesses, the rejections, the defamations, the injustices, the aloneness, all the "I should have's" and "I didn't do's." Pull out: bad
mother roots, bad father, not a good enough wife, husband,
worker. Pull them out. They are so invalid anyway.*

*Plant now the roses of Hope, Love, Promise, God
Consciousness, and the Glory of your Soul. In place of the ugly*

weeds of fear, the red and yellow roses start growing in great profusion. At one point, Jesus was called "The Rose." That is where the Rosicrucians got their name, the Society of the Rose Cross. When you're planting these roses, you're planting the symbol of Jesus. They grow in your heart, thornless and beautiful. The scent is heady. Now, you must tend this garden, because weeds grow daily, sometimes faster, because we're in a negative environment. But ask that if you should leave it unattended, your guides are put in charge. Put the Holy Spirit in charge. You'll get back to it, but it's nice to know that you have helpers there.

Feel your soul begin to rise up and magnify the Lord. Feel it rise. Feel the celebration within your heart; pull out all the pain. Feel the peace. Feel the hope. Feel the wellness and the inspiration.

Whenever anyone hurts you, visualize that feeling right in the middle of your solar plexus as a brilliant, huge, beautiful pink rose. Make this rose a symbol of your God Consciousness.

Cement your aura around you, white, gold, and purple lights sealing it. Nothing will harm you. No one can implant negativity. You are totally insulated. We are all linking together, creating a garland of roses. All of us are adding to each other's magnificent flower garden as a celebration to God.

We're saying, "God, I'm here before you today. I'm clean, pure of soul, clear of vision, clean of mind, and strong in my soul and judgment."

Become a prophet of good will; say to yourself, "I will go out and prophesize to make people free of guilt and fear and trepidation. I can come to you, God, without all the chains of fear. Unfettered, in a true heart, in a loving manner, to be myself. I am what I am. I am who I am."

Feel the grace now cascading over you. Take a deep breath and bring yourself up, all the way up, feeling absolutely marvelous.

This is your communion with God.

Tenet 4

Create your heaven, not a hell.
You are a creator made from God.

Milton and many other authors have said throughout the centuries: Within every man is a heaven and a hell. I think in our theological wanderings—whether it was St. Thomas Aquinas, St. Augustine, or even Sartre in his existentialism—we have tried to find out the truth about evil. And what did humanity do?

We *created* "hell." But that hell is where? Here. *This* planet is where hell is. There is no red-suited demon waiting for you in a pit. Trust me. What are we making of God? A cartoon, a caricature, or something from a children's story.

As you ascend higher to God, you become more selective of the people in your life. If God becomes your focus, you want to "fast-track" your soul's perfection. God is always present within all of us, but you have to ascend to Him. Climb that mountain of self and climb the man-made negativity in this world. The final ascent requires you to get out of yourself and ascend toward God and be chosen, because you choose God.

In discussions on the subject of judgment, I always ask, "Where did it come from?" I have to watch myself very carefully. Unless you're riding that dark horse along with a person, unless you're walking in their shoes, unless you know where their soul is, how do you have the right to go up and tell someone how wrong and bad they are, and that you are the judge of their soul? Where does the ego come in on this? I have a real problem judging.

I keep saying to myself every day, "I want to judge just the actions—not the soul." That's hard, isn't it? Because there are people who do awful, horrible things to others. Don't you think, in dark moments, *Boy, I'd like to slash and torture those people who hurt kids?* But you can't, can you? Give that forgiveness up to God. If you can't forgive the wrongdoers in the world, then ask God to forgive them for you.

People want to judge us. Then why don't they try walking a mile in our shoes? Francine says, "The only way you can ever judge anything is by the actions that live on after a person dies." What did that person create? Has there been nothing but pain and heartache and no help and no comfort?

Tenet 5
Turn thy power outward, not inward, for therein shines the Light and the Way.

Turn your power outward. Do you know why that works? *You smile.* If the eyes are windows to the soul, then the smile is the open door. You can smile with your eyes, but until your lips move, you don't open any door, do you? It's probably the one gesture of our whole body that puts out and does not take in. Do you realize that? All the others take in somehow, but this one is just pure light shining outward. Nothing is expected from that.

Nearly everyone will return a genuine smile. Even the meanest, crossest face—if you smile, they usually smile back. I remember when I was a little girl, I would get to church very early every morning. My dad had to drop me off at St. James Cathedral because we lived so far away. In those days, being in Catholic school, I wore the little beanie and the little plaid skirt. I was always in the front row.

I remember every morning I would watch this old lady with a black cloth coat and beautiful white hair walk up to the big crucifix, kneel down, walk across, and light a candle to the infant Jesus of Prague. Every morning I would watch her. Even as a child, I was very psychic about people. I knew she had a bad hip, and I knew how sad she was. Every morning she would walk by, and I would *smile* at her. This must have gone on for almost a whole school year.

One day she walked up to me, leaned over the pew, and said, "Your smile is the only thing that has kept me going in all the darkness. I've lost two sons. Your face, your smile in this dark church, is all I have left."

I thought then, *I can do that.* I kept that with me always—not just because I smiled at her, but because she gave me something back. I was so proud, so happy that day.

Turn your smile outward. Reach out that hand. That is what fingers are for. Reach toward each other and love each other. The time is so short, even if you live to be 80 years old. Wouldn't you rather be on the right side of things than the wrong side? Wouldn't you rather say, "I did it out of love. I did it out of caring. I helped as many people as I could," than to say, "I only took care of myself, just shot through life, and never created one bit of light. I never smiled. I was nothing but a meteor that streaked by."

You want to be a star that continuously shoots and sprays light like a firecracker.

Tenet 6

In faith, be like the wind chimes. Hold steady
until faith, like the wind, moves you to joy.

Sometimes, just don't move at all. Be perfectly still. That's why prayer is so important. Prayer is *talking* to God. Meditation is *listening to* Him.

Be *very still* sometimes. People often say, "Sylvia, I have no time to meditate." Then just sit down for a few minutes, take a deep breath, and say, "Okay, my intellect and emotion are cemented together. *Hit it, God.* Give me the message." It will come.

Your guides are always talking to you, but you aren't quiet enough. You haven't stilled your mind. You walk around with all that noise, rattle, commotion, and thoughts. Sometimes I have to say to myself, "Be still. Be quiet. My heart is beating. I'm breathing. I'm sweeping the corridors of my mind, literally, with a white broom."

The next thing that comes down the corridor of my mind is a message, which I accept. Many say they never get any reciprocity from God, but that's because we don't listen. Whenever you get a sudden, brilliant idea, then thank God for it.

I've said to people, "Don't travel in a blue car this year." They will come back to me six months later, and say, "I had a terrible car crash in a friend's blue car." I'm on a human plane, and so are you, so we make mistakes.

So many mothers will say, "I told my kids not to do that. I told them 50 times." Did they hear you? No. How many times have you counseled a friend, "He's no good." Do they listen? No. Why do we expect to hear God? We don't even hear each other. We don't even hear ourselves talk. If we did, some of us would shut up.

Tenet 7
Know that each life is a path winding toward perfection.
It is the step after step that is hard, not the whole of the journey.

When you stop and look back over the whole of your journey, it doesn't seem all that bad, does it? Look back. I want you to do that today. Take 20 minutes and do a quick overview of your life. It's a wonderful meditation. I want you to pick out all the bright spots. When you look back over the near misses and the horrors, see how dim they are.

For example, at the time that Abraham Lincoln was killed, it was a national tragedy. But as time passed, people began to make jokes about John Wilkes Booth. What happens as you look back on a bad marriage, or on any sorrow? It begins to diminish, layer by layer, so that you can view it, see it, and talk about it without pain. When you're too close, the razor cuts you, doesn't it?

All of life is a journey. Say to yourself, "I'm just going to get through it, then I get to go Home." You *will* get home—to the Other Side. You may be stranded by the road just now with no tires and no gas, but you will, eventually, get Home, even if you have to walk. When you do, there will be somebody to love you, hold you, and cocoon you. There will be parties to go to, loved ones to see, and reunions to be enjoyed. That's what we do on the Other Side. But you don't help anyone by being a crabby nightmare as you walk down the road.

Is there anything worse than being with somebody who is always cranky, upset, and griping all the time, complaining, "I thought it would be better than this." Who told you it was going to be easy? Who told you it would be a picnic? No one.

On the Other Side, they said, "Go down the chute and handle it," didn't they? They didn't give us a warm coat and a first-aid kit. They said, "Go down, and survive the mess."

Do not gripe about it. That is such negativity: "I want it to be better. I wanted this. I wanted that." Sure you did. We all wanted to be wealthy and good-looking, have our children turn out perfectly, and have a wonderful marriage. We all wanted to run to the beach, grab a prince, and ride off on a white horse, didn't we? We all wanted that. We all believed it. When we were little girls and little boys, we were all going to grow up and be strong, beautiful, wealthy, and happy, and have great marriages. We were going to be honest, religious, and true. Well, most of us didn't get there, did we? But that's okay.

We have ourselves, we have each other, and more important, we have God. Gnosticism is an individual thread that becomes a rope by each one of us taking their strand and winding it with others. I want each one of you to mentally take your strand and wind it so that the rope gets bigger and bigger. You know why? If the cord gets stronger, then other people can pull on it.

Gnosticism is a rope and a cart. It knows exactly where it's going, even if some of us who jumped on the cart don't know. Gnosticism is the Way, the Truth, and the Light.

Stop and think about that. For example, some would say that my grandmother, Ada, was "saddled with" a son who had cerebral palsy. From the time he was born, he couldn't do things that other people could do. Yet he had a wonderful mind. So for all the 52 years of his life, Ada took care of him. We all called him "Brother."

I used to ask her, "Grandma, I love Brother with all my heart— but isn't it difficult to care for him?" She said, "No, no. It's just one step at a time when I look back over it." Isn't that true? When we look back over difficult labors or losing a job or any other painful thing, does it really matter that much? If we could get ourselves *above* the body and *not into* the body, we'd realize that all this passes away eventually. Grit your teeth and just go through it. Don't fall over. Don't stop.

Now you ask, "Well, what about resting?" That's fine. Falling over or giving up is something else. You say, "I don't want to do this." Don't you think there are some mornings that all of us, including myself, don't want to get up? We don't want to do it, do we? You put your feet over the side of the bed, and you say, "Oh, no, *no*. I don't want to do this again."

But that is what life is, a daily decision to continue. The big events in life, the crises, we can pretty much handle. But you know what really gets us? The pinpricks of everyday nit-picky things. The fact that you cannot be alone or have peace of mind, or you cannot get away from your own body or mind. That's what's so tough. Haven't you ever wanted to take a vacation from *yourself?*

When that happens, take a deep breath, put the white light of the Holy Spirit around you, and say, "I'm going to get through this one, too." What do they tell us when we're having a baby or surgery? "You *will* get through this." And you did, didn't you? That's what life is—a constant flow of *incisions* to get rid of this, get rid of that, cut this away, hone that down, take that out.

Realize that, and say, "Yes, I, too, will survive this." Because the God inside you, the God Consciousness, the Holy Spirit, will not let you fall, if you hang on to that cord firmly. Try to keep your mood up. That's so important. Nobody wants to be around someone who's miserable.

If you're miserable, nobody should know it. That doesn't mean you should keep hostility locked in, because that causes illness. But don't always be negative. Negativity breeds on itself, and it's very powerful on this side. We will occasionally get negative, down, depressed, and mean. And what happens? We want to know why everybody *else* is nasty and depressed. Unfortunately, we caused it. That's not guilt; that's a fact. Negativity spreads like a mental virus.

Take it one step at a time. We've heard that so many times, haven't we? One step, one hour, one day. We're so busy worrying about what's going to happen tomorrow that we don't enjoy today.

STAR MEDITATION

I want you to put your hands upward on your thighs and take a deep breath. See behind your eyes a beautiful, glowing star in a night sky. This star is blue, with shoots of red, white, and silver around the corners. Now we're not just looking at it; we are part *of it.*

This star, inside us, is emanating the magnitude of our soul—our greatness, beauty, and perfection. It is radiating. The beautiful points of the star are pushing out any and all negativity. To an outside viewer, it might look as if we were streaking, but we're gently descending in a dark sky.

At first, during our descent, we're feeling very afraid, all alone, and somehow lost. But hush. In the dark sky, we seem to feel the refraction of another light. We look over, and there is another star that seems to be falling along with us. Now, above us there are more stars. And lo and behold—as we turn our head and look behind us—there are lots of stars falling with us.

Now, we know that our star does not intercept the light of the others, and we are falling together. We are all radiating our love of God, right action, nonjudgment, and even a feeling of acceptance. We are streaking across this dark world with the light. The stars now seem to fall together. If you were to stand back, you would hear little cries of happiness because of the big, huge light we make together.

Then still more stars are joining our cluster. We feel the bond of our starlight as we fall together in the night sky, even like the star of Bethlehem showing the way, the truth, and the light. Feel yourself content and peaceful; feel strength of will and a sound judgment center. Feel the strength of your courage, able to endure the "slings and arrows of outrageous fortune." Feel the quiet peace.

Feel the grace bestowed upon you from Father God, Mother Azna, and the Holy Spirit that surrounds us. From today

*onward, have peace in your heart. Share your thread of truth
for others who are seeking.*
    Bring yourself up.

Tenet 8

*Be simple. Allow no man to judge you, not even yourself,
for you cannot judge God.*

I love that. Be simple. People say, "What does that mean—simple-minded?" Of course not. *Simple* means "not complex, the pure essence." All the behavioral overlays are cut away.

Allow no one to judge you, not even yourself. Here is the most important part—this is where we all get hung up in human form. You cannot judge yourself. Many times each day we say to ourselves, even if we don't verbalize it, "What made me do that? That was mean. I shouldn't have done that. If only I was a better father (or mother or sister or husband or wife)."

Your chart is set. You wrote the silly chart. We all wrote these insane charts in order to graduate. So now we're down here, and we have to go through with it. But don't judge yourself or feel that you're not the "right" person. Remember, you were *supposed* to be the way you are so that somebody else could perfect in spite of you—as long as you intended no harm. That stipulation is all-important.

If we are constantly mean and always wishing that people were dead for no good reason, then that's a different thing entirely. That gets into the realm of *insanity*. Most human beings do not wish harm on another person unless *they've* been harmed, which is just part of getting over something. Then you get over it and don't think about it anymore. How long can you hate your ex-husband or your mother? It gets to be *boring* after a while.

To judge yourself comes at an enormous cost to you. It destroys your self-esteem. People say, "I was married to so-and-so, and it destroyed my self-esteem." No, no. *You* gave them the bludgeon to hit you. My first marriage was like that, if you read my biography.

Well, you do either one thing or the other. Either allow the abuse to continue, or you move away from it, mentally or physically. My ex-husband's words ran off my back, even though they hurt, but when he started on the children, I said, "That's the end of it."

No one destroys you except yourself. Do you know what's so awful about these dark, lousy entities that run around? They know where your weakness is. They are psychic in the *wrong* sense. They knife you, after you give them the knife. I've done this. We give them all our weaknesses, and they use them against us.

Don't let anybody judge you. Consider this: No one can judge God, yet all of us *are* God. No one can judge that part of God in someone that is experiencing. The human weaknesses are just part of living, part of existing. All suffering is transient, as is life, which is why it's so much nicer to have a pleasant outlook about the whole thing. You *will* get over everything, even life.

My grandmother used to say, "Who's going to care a hundred years from now?" Nobody will, because we won't be here. Nobody. Who's going to care two weeks from now?

Please be kind to each other. In that, you are leaving yourself open for returned kindness. That doesn't mean you can't vent your feelings and get mad and angry. But, especially, *be kind to yourself.* Do not judge that God-center that is inside of you.

Tenet 9
You are a light in a lonely, dark desert, enlightening many.

This is central to the Gnostic purpose of life. We really are meant to be lights in a dark and lonely world. I hear people saying, "This philosophy changed my life."

Each of us is a little tiny light all over the world, and together we are becoming a very large sparkler for all to see. As open and as wide as this world is, and considering how much darkness surrounds us, even our small lights seem like a searchlight.

Tenet 10

Let no one convince you that you are
less than a God. Do not let fear imprison your spiritual growth.

Do you know how much of our lives are ruled by fear? Do you know what our biggest fear is? Some say it is the fear of darkness or fear of falling. No. No. Our greatest fear is the fear of acceptance. That's what keeps us hindered, every single day of our life, in some form or another. We say, "I don't want to look stupid. I don't want anybody to think badly of me. I don't want to be too obvious. I don't want to be too subliminal. I don't want to be too martyred." It is constant, ongoing *worry*.

You are God. You are part of God. We are each a finger on the hand of God, although we each experience life differently. You can't let anybody step on you. The splendor of your own inner God Consciousness must rise up. There is no one anywhere that is you. You are unique in all of creation.

Your fear should cease when you stop and think: *We are all going to die.* You may feel that to be morbid, but it's not. Between life and death is all you have to worry about. Living is a lot of worry because you're constantly struggling. Have you ever looked into babies' eyes? It's like they're saying, "What the hell am I doing here again? This is really depressing."

When a loved one is nearing death, the best thing we can say to them is, "Listen. You have completed your work. Let go now; we will all be fine. It's been wonderful having you with us for a while. We will all be over pretty soon." You bet we will. There's no other option.

In addition, we have a terrible fear that when we get over to the Other Side and scan our life, we are going to sit there and say, "Oh, no. What a big failure I was." Trust me: You won't think any of that. What you see when you scan your life are the good acts, the loving things that you did, the people that you helped. The person who yelled at you doesn't mean anything, nor does your job, your bum car, or the fact that you never got married. These things seem important now, but they mean nothing when you're over there with all your loved ones. You forget all the little things. You say, "God, that was a mess. I'm so happy it's over with."

Tenet 11
*Do not allow the unfounded belief in demons to
block your communion with God.*

I'm in such a rampage over this. Let me explain a sad truth: To bring more money in, religious organizations throw the concept of satan, hell, and demons down our throats. Don't you see how easy it is? "We don't have to talk about theology; we need no books to reference. If I tell you from my pulpit that a demon is going to get you, that settles it. According to me, satan is going to get your immortal soul—unless I save you."

If you are really thoughtful, read the Bible analytically. The "devil" is only spoken of *three times.* Once he comes in the form of a snake, simply to contradict the Egyptians, to whom the snake was a fertility god. The third time he shows up is in John's psychotic dream, *Revelations,* which was not added until 500 years afterward. So forget that crazy thing.

The second appearance of satan is in the Book of Job. God is speaking with Lucifer like they're old friends: "You can do anything to Job, but you cannot kill him." In the Orthodox Judaism of that day, death was the worst thing that could happen to you. I've studied the Book of Job, which is a beautiful form of prose. The way the protagonist and antagonist speak to each other is almost poetic—the dark side of humanity speaking to the light side, all in parables, allegory, and hyperboles.

When Jesus spoke to the masses, it was inevitable that there would be some misunderstandings, that some things would pass down erroneously from the oral tradition. An example is the symbol of the snake. It's odd because the snake that's so bad in Genesis shows up again as the huge, bronze serpents in front of King Solomon's temple. If snakes were so evil, why were they on the temple?

Can you imagine a loving God creating a hell? It's not possible. You can't have a loving God and a mean God all in one. I taught in a Catholic school for 17 years. Oh, the nervous breakdowns that I saw. I thought, *If this is so good, then why are there so many nervous breakdowns and so much dissension?* But this was really heavy-duty stuff: The devil was always present. They talked about it, keeping it alive and well. Negativity breeds on itself.

Get rid of that silly "devil" stuff in your life. It's archaic and stupid. You're too intelligent to believe in a red suit and horns and nonsense like that. In ancient times, people in all cultures believed that demons caused illness and so forth because they were ignorant of viruses. We simply know better now.

Tenet 12

The body is a living temple unto God, wherein we worship the spark of the Divine.

The more we realize this, the better we will feel. God can cure and heal as long as your Divine spark can rise up to God. Be sure you don't poison your body, as that will destroy your connection. You can't drink heavily or take drugs and hope that your God-center will rise up.

I think that people sometimes try to numb their God-center through abuse of one sort or another. When that inner voice speaks, sometimes we don't want to hear it. We fear what it might say, which we believe could make our lives even harder. However, it really is *easier* when the spirit of your true self rises up, to instill some pride about yourself.

Regarding people who don't live to get older, you often hear, "Oh, isn't that a shame. They were only here for 15 years." Sure we miss them, but they just went Home early. Why does anybody want to keep them here? For selfish reasons, of course. I say to people who have lost someone, "Are *you* having such a great time?"

"No," they say. "My life has been terribly hard."

"Then why do you want them here?"

"Because they had their whole life ahead of them."

And you would want them to continuing suffering a life of pain? All of life is temporary.

Some stay down here for the whole training period, and some do not. What difference does it make? You, too, are going to get there, but in the meantime, try to take care of the body as well as you can. You don't need to be obsessive, but try to get a little exercise, eat right, and live healthy. We know within ourselves what keeps us healthy. We know when we don't get enough exercise, when we stress too much, and so forth. If you impair the body, then your mind and soul function poorly. Can you meditate when you're sick? You cannot. We should meditate *before* we get sick.

Tenet 13
God does not create the adversities in life.
By your own choice, they exist to aid in your perfection.

God created the school for us, but we chart our lessons. You even filled in the *blanks*. It's important to remember that when we feel disconnected from God and think that life has no purpose, even those feelings are there for our spiritual growth.

You wrote the script, and you're going to live it, whether you like it or not. You better smile through it, because you're going to complete it.

Certainly there have been times when I said, "I don't want to do this." Guess what? I did it anyway. You will, too. The best thing to do, like giving birth, is bear down and do it. Be firm, be courageous, be strong, and know in your heart how proud God is of you.

Gnosticism may seem to be unstructured; this is because there is no dogma. However, there are rules that reside universally within everyone's soul. The personal truth that I live by may not be the same truth that others follow, but each path is a valid means to spirituality.

No one can judge morality, just as we never judge someone's soul.

We know that there are "dark" entities who can invade and upset our lives, but they can't possess us. They are there for us to learn from.

We must have a place to go in which we can grab each other's hand, help each other, give, love, and know that someone else is walking along with us. This is what churches originally were *supposed* to be. Father Erwin told me years ago, "Sylvia, you're doing what churches should have been doing—*administering to the people.*"

Tenet 14
Karma is nothing more than honing the wheel of evolvement. It is not retribution, but merely a balancing of personal and universal experience.

Please do not let anybody tell you that the reason they remain in an abusive relationship is due to their karma. *Do not use that kind of silly excuse.* The etymology of the word *karma* goes clear back to the ancient Hindus. Karma is nothing more than the soul's experiencing for its own perfection, your individual perfection.

You will come into this life as a male or a female. Most entities maintain a specific sexual identify, but you may switch it on occasion. Many times that is the basis for homosexuality. If I've had 50 lives as a female, then suddenly come in as a male, what do you think my sexual preference is going to be? There is no judgment here. Didn't I pick a life as a Catholic/Jewish girl so that I could deal with prejudice? Or why pick a life in a subjugated race, such as black or red? Only *strong souls* pick that.

I've often said to people, "If you think you're so superior, go to another country where your skin color or language is in the minority. See how much you don't know, and experience what you feel about prejudice or racism." Until we group together as one total entity and have a feeling of unity, we're never going to have peace. We've got to stop all prejudice and bigotry.

We can judge actions, but not individuals. Our soul is here to evolve karmically and gain perfection through our own experience.

Every time you think you've learned a pattern, you have to face it again. How many times have we done it? You finally get away from the wrong person, then you find yourself in exactly the same situation again. You say, "Doesn't this feel familiar, this same bed of nails?"

Of course it does. You just traded it for sharper nails. You don't get out of this life without "paying dues." There's no way out of it.

It's so amazing. We fear facing our fears more than going through them. Do you know how much we fear injections? We get to the doctors and we make more noise and pain for ourselves. When it's over and done, we say, "Oh, that wasn't so bad."

It's the "unknown" of life that we fear. What's the worst thing that can happen? You die? Big deal—that's the easiest part of it all. It's *living* that's so tough. This doesn't mean that we don't love life. Of course we do. "Life is a banquet," as Rosalind Russell's character said in *Auntie Mame*.

You should take from the banquet what you want, but choose carefully. Do *not* let people tell you that it's your karma that you have to stay in a nightmarish marriage or job. Karma is a different thing. When a situation begins to wreck you, *you must leave*.

Tenet 15
God allows each person the opportunity for perfection,
whether you need one life or a hundred to reach your goal.

I find this to be the most amazingly understandable and logical concept in support of an all-loving God. I did not always believe it was true until I proved it to myself. Think of a *logical* God. He must be logical—He has to be *perfect,* doesn't He? Why would He give us just one chance to perfect our soul? We get *lots* of chances. Do you know why? God experiences through us. He is wonderful, perfect, and all-loving.

Never believe in a vengeful god. That is not our loving God, but only a falsehood. Talk about idolatry—it is idolatrous to fear God. You should love Him. God is all love. Think of your own love for your children, then think about God's love, which is magnified trillions of times more.

We are *all* sons and daughters of God. Every single one of us carries the Divine. Everyone knows the truth. You have the God Consciousness within you, which is connected directly to the absolute truth.

You have a beauty and uniqueness that is found nowhere else in any universe. No one has the right to control your search for truth. No one has the right to tell you that you cannot know God's plan. The minute you hear that, there's a hidden agenda. God made His truth available for every single person. If that is not so—stop and think and be reasonable—then God plays favorites? God does *not* play favorites. Not my God. He does *not* love only one group. That concept was designed by man to control others through fear.

Tenet 16

Devote your life, your soul, your very existence, to
the service of God. For only there will you find meaning in life.

This doesn't mean that you have to be a nun, a priest, a monk, a rabbi, a holy person, or any such person. Those of us who have done so *chose* to dedicate their lives to God. Does that mean never having a good time? A bunch of us went out the other night and we had a fabulous time. We attended a show and went out to eat. We *do not* walk around wearing sad faces in sackcloth and ashes. The main distinction is the commitment within our soul that we will devote our life to the real meaning of the Mother Goddess, the Father God, and the love of God.

This whole world was created so that people could learn about the nature of their souls. That's all it is. It's like, "There are a lot of bad schools here. We're trying to get a good school going." With a proper education, it's easier to make the transition to the Other Side.

Keep this in your heart: Every day you're going to do something good for someone. This does *not* mean that you're going to let people take advantage of you or that you'll be a submissive fool who says, "Whatever you want to do, slap me in the face. Fine. God love you." *No.* If someone slaps you in the face, you slap them back. You do not let anybody step on your dignity.

Don't let anybody defile your temple. You *can* have a temper. You do not have to let people hurt you. Jesus didn't. Why have we forgotten that he had a temper? He took a whip to the "money changers" at the temple. He said, "How dare you defile a temple." We seem to forget that side of Jesus. Why do we let people hurt us so badly? Why do we live with guilt? If we embrace our God-center, knowing that God is with us, we lose all that guilt and submissive behavior.

Tenet 17
War is profane. Defense is compulsory.

We believe that inciting war is wrong. At heart, we are really conscientious objectors, and not just with respect to war in the traditional sense, but to battles of every kind. We *do* believe in defending our own sovereignty, only if it comes to the point of being on our own ground or person. We do not believe in going elsewhere to defend ideology.

SUN MEDITATION

Put your hands upward on your thighs. Take a deep breath, close your eyes, and visualize the white light of the Holy Spirit around you. I want you to get rid of some of this stress that you deal with all the time in your schools, jobs, and homes.

Take a deep breath. Concentrate on the white light around you. Notice that your breathing is becoming calm and very regular. Pay attention to your chest rising and falling, gently exhaling all the negativity you collected during the day.

When you inhale, pull in God's pure light, the light of the

God Consciousness, and the pink light of Azna the Mother God, who is the other side of the Father God, completing the duality. Your inner duality, your intellect and emotion, will be cemented together right now.

All of a sudden, I want you to feel yourself, the totality of your own soul, being lifted by the power of God into a beautiful blue sky. The sun is warm. As it hits you, all the stress, all the pain, all the addictions, and all the negatives that you carry (needing an extra pill or drink or whatever) are released. Let all those bodily crutches go.

Feel the warmth of the sun now flowing into your mind and cleansing out all the dark places of anxiety. Your breathing is calm and regular. Let go of all prejudices, all hurts, all ingratitudes. Let them go. Now, let your shoulders shrug. Feel all the systems of your body relaxing. Your blood pressure normalizes, and your heartbeat becomes regular.

Feel the grace of the God Consciousness in your soul. Feel the Holy Spirit descending upon you. Feel a sense of righteousness rising up within your soul. You know yourself to be good and kind and well meaning. All these other things that you have carried are nothing but behavioral overlays; they are not you.

Now, while you're floating, feel that your aura expands outward and fills the world. Let us pray in our hearts for all the people who are sick or dying or homeless. People with AIDS. All the people suffering in civil wars and genocides everywhere. Wherever there is pestilence or greed or avarice, pray for them. We ask for the power of God to come and make us well.

We ask for alleviation from our enemies. We ask that all those be purified who do not understand our way. We ask for mirrors to surround all of us, reflecting outward so that all negativity will be reflected back to the person who sends it. No evil to be done—just reflect back what they're doing to us through adversity, through the lies told about us through all the hurts, in order to neutralize our pain and make our enemies go on their way.

Feel yourself floating now in this beautiful, brilliant sky of blue. Feel that all the garbage of life is falling away from you. You become lighter and lighter. Ascend higher and higher, knowing that you are loved. All of a sudden, as you're floating, feel people who love you start coming closer, floating toward you, and each hand reaches out. Each time the fingertips touch other fingertips, you become electrified by more Godliness, more spirituality, more love.

Jesus spoke about two or more being gathered together in his name. But there are many more of us than two. For the love of God, and the way Jesus wanted us to live, is our commitment.

Feel yourself now coming back to yourself. Carry the glowing feeling with you. The spirit of Novus Spiritus is the divine spirit breathing the divine spirit. We ask this in the name of the Mother God, the Father God, the God Consciousness, and the Holy Spirit within you.

Tenet 18

Death is the act of returning Home.
It should be done with grace and dignity.
You may preserve that dignity by refusing prolonged use of artificial life-support systems. Let God's will be done.

You wonder exactly how to accomplish this? If you really want it this way, that is the way it will happen. This final tenet says that you *do not* have to suffer, but this does not mean taking your own life. You don't have to be kept alive via artificial means. Right now, in your heart, make a Living Will that says that when it's your time, you'll let go of the cord and return Home easily.

There is nothing worse than outstaying your welcome. I say to people, "Go Home." People ask me so many times, "What is the meaning of life?" It is to do good, love and help as many people as you can, and then shut up and go Home. That is the meaning of life— if you do that, you've done it all. You say, "Yes, but I haven't accomplished anything." I ask, "Have you done anything really bad and mean and hateful?" "No." Then you *have done it.* You have walked through the nightmare of life. At the base core, it is a "hell" here. That doesn't mean we don't love life, but the majority of it is hard. But then there *is* some beauty. Every once in a while, the curtain parts, and a little bit of the Other Side comes through.

Do you know why we walk around with an "empty feeling" all the time? It's because we're so homesick for the Other Side, where everything, truly, is so beautiful and wonderful. There is no adversity, no illness, no fear, and no hate.

Then somebody says, "Then let's all go get this wonderfulness right now." No, because you must finish your chart. If you leave too early, you'll have to come back and go through the whole nightmare again.

You may preserve dignity by refusing prolonged use of artificial life-support systems. Let God's will be done. There comes a time when the soul's dignity is to be preserved *at all costs.* A person has the right to go with dignity, without all that noisy agony.

I hope the tenets of my church have resonated in your soul as "right." I always tell people to take what feels right to them, and leave the rest behind. This church has been in my heart for decades. It really began to solidify in 1986 when I took a big step.

I stepped out on the stage in 1986 at De Anza College in Cupertino, California, and said, "I am going to start a new religion." I could feel the emotional ripple in the audience: "Now what is this crazy thing?" But I persevered and created Novus Spiritus as my personal testament to our all-loving God. Now we have a wonderful church where people are healed, souls are repaired, and God is put in charge of our lives.

People say, "My mind got better. I'm not depressed anymore. I can make it through the week." That's what church was meant for.

You *must* carry that light. You are charged to carry it for God. If we don't rid the world of darkness, we haven't done much good.

Because if you give light to someone, guess what happens? It reflects.

At the root of everything that is bad, you will find the word *greed*. It is one of those primordial flaws that comes with the flesh. On the Other Side, there is no greed. Once we learn to rule out greed, then the positive is allowed to come in.

Now, what is the primary emotion that blocks God's love from coming through? Fear. Fear seems to rule our lives, whether consciously or insidiously, if we allow it to. "I'm afraid to fly," people say. "I'm afraid to drive over a bridge. I'm afraid I'm going to get sick. I'm afraid I won't have enough money. I'm afraid no one will love me." Whether we realize it or not, those seeds grow without limit.

Start by disciplining your minds to think. Be scrupulous about this just for a little while, because we are certainly scrupulous about everything else, aren't we? We analyze. We cling to fears as precious gems, don't we? We fear that we're going to die. Yes, you are. Big deal. That's one thing you can be assured of.

"I'm afraid of dying without finishing what I started." What are you talking about? You will finish on the Other Side if you don't finish here. What if you wanted to be a dancer and you couldn't be? Guess what? You *are* one on the Other Side. You can also write on the Other Side, you research, you love animals, you help souls transition into life. You do all the things that you want to do. Sometimes when children first come over, they stay children for a while. Just like when the elderly come over, they stay elderly for a while. It's too much of a shock to the system. What if you're 89 years old, and suddenly you find yourself going through the tunnel at age 30? The mind needs some time to adjust.

Guess what? *Everyone's* life is miserable. Don't tell me that great chunks of life aren't miserable, because they are. Of course, you chose a certain amount of misery, but the learning is from how you handle it. Think of yourself as going down a dark hallway, because sometimes life has these dark hallways. Then just run as fast as possible through the hallway until you again reach the light.

You don't have to spend your life alone. Go out and be with people. Help them. People have said to me, "I have no friends." I've told them, "Then you're not a friend."

People say, "I have no one that loves me." Who do *you* love? That is most important. You see, there is only so much space inside that can be occupied. If you have all of it filled with love and positivism, then negativity cannot get in. Besides, two emotions cannot occupy the same space. I don't care what you say. You can't be truly miserable and truly happy at the same time. It can't be, unless you're schizophrenic, which can also be dealt with. Bittersweet emotions are not what I'm talking about.

Here's another important thing. Be sure that you're a conduit for God. Do you know what a conduit is? Anything that conducts or flows. It can be electrical or it can be a piece of pipe, but it conducts energy. Always be a source of God's love, and let it flow freely to all you meet.

Did you ever see anything in your life like what is coming out on psychic phenomena on TV? The world is seeking new answers because religion has not answered the needs of our soul. Humanity is saying, "I want to love God; I want to follow His path; I want to get through this life; I want to go Home."

Yet change the channel, and you can still find crazy evangelists playing on our fears. They get everybody agitated, saying, "Jesus saves. Fear God; you are damned to Hell." That's mob violence. Fear. That's an ugly, ugly emotion. Love is what Jesus came to show us.

If I give you love and you give me love and everyone gives each other love, no one can control another. No one. Then God's love is the conduit.

"But what if the world ends?" I've said to so many people. "What if I told you right now that in two minutes, the world is going to end? What would you do, truthfully? You should sit still, first of all. Many people say, though, "I would call my kids." Why? They're going to be in the tunnel with you in two minutes. The only bad thing about this is that we'll all be in the tunnel at the same time, and it's going to be crowded.

People say, "What if there's a nuclear holocaust?" There won't be, but what if there was? Not that life isn't precious, but it's only a school that, naturally, we don't want to see destroyed. We don't. But after you graduate, how many of you during the day think of your high school? Your grade school? It's a vague memory unless you're still in it, isn't it? Do you think when we get to the Other Side that this world will be our whole focus?

Even Jesus showed fear, didn't he, at Gethsemane? When he was kneeling there, he looked up and said, "Please, please. Remove this chalice from me." He knew that his life was taking a bend. He was hoping, trust me, that Gnosticism would flourish, and that he could stay in his own land. Then what did he say? He replied with, "Thy will be done."

In your fear, say, "Thy will be done," because your will and God's will cannot be different. For a week, think, *How many times do I have fear? Even the little, tiny fears?* Even the negative things of, "Oh my God, I have nothing for dinner tonight." Move through your day as a joy, not as a dark tunnel in which you have to keep constantly turning on lights to illuminate your soul.

Regardless of what church you go to, do not let them force the Bible on you, scream at you, tell you that God does not love you, or that you're a sinner. If you do, you have now replaced the true God for a false God, and illness creeps in. Think to yourself how many times you've been bound by fear and anxiety. What happens? You get sick, don't you? I don't mean just necessarily physically sick, but soul-sick. Then depression sets in. And do you know what happens? We spiral down: "No one loves me; everybody hates me. I have no friends; it's been a miserable life. I don't feel good; I'm getting older."

Instead of saying, "Yes, I am. I've paid my dues. I'm proud of it, and pretty soon I'm going to go Home," isn't it so much nicer to go down the white tunnel toward Home and say, "Gee, I wasn't a mess; I didn't whine and mumble and be miserable or complaining my whole way down."

Do not be humble. Is there anything worse than overt humility? Stand tall. Be proud, because you are descended from Mother and Father God. You are their offspring, not just Jesus. We are all messengers on this planet. Because one person stands out, it doesn't mean that you're diminished by that.

Somehow I wrote that I wanted to be the big mouth and have a burning purpose. I used to think sometimes, in the darkness of my own fear, *Will anyone ever become alive with this belief that I have? Will anyone come out and share this mission with me? Will I be alone crying in a lonely desert, saying, "God loves you. God is good. Mother God is with you. God Consciousness is there"?*

For a long time, I *did* feel alone. But if you live it long enough, then your belief becomes a reality, and people from far away begin to hear a message on the airwaves. They hear you, and they come.

Gnostics have always been a *phenomenon*. They did not use a lot of texts because they were mostly concerned with how you live, who you are, and what you're becoming for God. A lot of the writings were destroyed for political reasons. But when we speak, we're bringing forward old, forgotten knowledge.

If you don't go deeper into Gnosticism, I hope that within your heart you carry a piece of us—the ministers, the love we give, the testimonies that you can hear, and the healing that you can have. Without fear. Without being held onto. Without cultism. Just touch us, and then go out and light another light. For that one act, your darkness will be diminished.

GOLDEN SWORD MEDITATION

Surround yourself today with a beautiful, shimmering, golden light. As it expands, feel yourself sitting in the midst of this golden light. Feel it breathing and pulsating around you.

In front of you stands the female Mother side of God, and the male Father side of God. Azna, the Mother Goddess, hands you a golden sword. When you reach out and bring it to you, against the golden light it looks like a crucifix. You wield the sword and cut through all fear in your heart and soul, removing the offending pain and releasing grief and guilt.

Still sitting in the golden light, begin to feel—first shadowy and then more solid—all the loved ones who have passed before, beginning to move behind you. All the people whom you have known from the Other Side in any life who have loved you, and whom you have loved. Your spirit guide stands behind you, your backup support system.

You feel the grace now flowing from the front to the back. With this protection, how could you ever feel fear or aloneness? As these marvelous entities crowd around you, you feel the transfer of energy. You make a pact today, with God and yourself, that you will release fear and any vestiges of greed. You will not be a conduit for someone else's greed or fear.

You are self-contained. You are in control of your life, your heart, your mind, your soul, and your body. You allow no person to divert you from your path. You are self-contained. Now you feel total help and love flowing around you.

Take a deep breath. Keep this image, and feel protected through all the days of your life. Bring yourself all the way up, feeling absolutely marvelous, better than you have ever felt before.

Living Without Fear

Benjamin Franklin said that fear was always expecting that you would be exposed. Now stop and think about that for a few minutes. Being exposed. How? I think it has to do with fearing that our vulnerability will become apparent.

In other words, "If I love you too much," said the poet, "will you hurt me too deeply? If I give too much to you, will I have anything come back? If you really know my face, will you not reject me?" We spend so much of our lives living behind both faces, don't we? Not because we are deceptive, but because we're so afraid of exposing ourselves to hurt. Fear keeps you from spiritual growth. It keep you from growing in any way. Our fears and phobias are what cripple us.

Yet, in Novus Spiritus, we don't have that fear. Every day we are replacing fear with unconditional love, saying, "You can be whatever you are, whatever you were, whatever you will be, and this church will love you." We accept both universal and personal truth.

This spiritual movement is to make you well, and let you go out and spread the word. There is a universal truth called "the law of the circle." What goes around, comes around. That's true, but how about an individual truth such as "You made me mad, and I'll get you for it"?

How do we reconcile these two truths? Begin to slowly allow the individual truths to drop away. When you get higher into the elevation of the spirit, the universal and the personal become the same. We let go of all the petty things.

So what does it matter if your child has a smart mouth? Is that a universal truth? Somebody might look at it as cute, but you may see it as hurt. But what if a child kills a parent? We all feel that in our souls. That is the universal truth of wrong. See what I'm saying? Drop the small stuff of life and be true to the spiritual aspects of life. More important, if you don't stop a wrong being done to you, that wrong will keep repeating itself.

Be a giver of universal truths. This is not to judge. We can judge actions, but we cannot judge the soul. Righteous anger should rise up, but only when your soul has been wronged.

If you don't have righteous anger, then you'll have fear. You cannot allow people to step on you. Even your own families can hurt you badly. So give warning signals: "You're now hurting me; that upsets me. I don't want you to do that again to me." If that doesn't do it, then remove yourself. You say, "Oh, but Sylvia, that is harsh." Yet it's better than swallowing it, and getting ill.

The one thing that Gnostic Christians have always done is researched and found truth. We ferret out the right, the just, the soul truth, which in every single person is their own knowledge of God without any trappings of fear. Consider the true message in the Biblical story of David and Goliath. David slew our fear. Let's make our giant fears into things that, today, we can slay.

Life is a process by which we overcome our fears. What have you done so bad, ever, that someone else has not done in some life? We've all done everything, haven't we? Hope to God that we've tried it all. We've been every color and every creed, because we had to be.

We come to the end of our road and look back and say, "I felt and experienced all this for God. Hopefully now, as a seeker of truth, I will merge my individual truth to the universal truth of what God wants. I will bear tidings of love and forgiveness and unconditional love."

Just live, my dear friends. Just live. It will all fall into place.

In the olden days, Mother God would bestow gratuities through all the year, and give Her blessing to all petitions that were given. On the day of the summer equinox, things were supposed to be given back. People used to bring food and clothing and harvest items.

We are so in need of giving back to Her the love and gratitude of what She has given us. I don't know about the rest of you, but I bet when you ask Her for something, you get it. Out of 20 things that I ask of Her, 19 come true for me. So there's a benefit here. But note, if we take, we have to give. That is the law of the circle.

No Fear Meditation

Please put your hands upward on your thighs. I want you to take a deep breath. Feel all sense of fear leaving. I want you to feel the white light of the Holy Spirit, the golden light of Jesus, the purple light of God around you, and the beautiful rose light of Azna descending over you.

Feel the fear and the prejudices and the cores of pain that spiral like darkness in your soul, pulled out like plugs. Feel the healing light going through every single cell of your body, searching out pain.

The beautiful lights keep swirling through, making your soul well, healing you, giving you the fire of the Holy Spirit to go out and be an example—an example of light.

Let go of the transgressions that have been done to you. If you've gone through your anger and your periods of unforgiveness, now let those plugs come out. Let all the dirty water run down the drain.

Give it to God. Let Him be the forgiver, so you can be free. Be steadfast, be loyal, be cognizant, be watchful, be healed. Let this spirit move through your body today and into your hands; as they are upward, they feel hot and glowing.

We are asking now for the healing power of the Holy Spirit, Jesus, and Azna to come. Your hands are hot as the spirit of healing comes through you. Everyone that you touch, everyone that brushes against your aura, everyone that comes in contact with you will be healed. We ask for this gift today.

Feel your hands get warmer. Feel how they pulsate. Feel that you can now put your hands upon yourself and heal yourself. You've been given the gift of healing.

Ask for the gifts of prophecy and enlightenment. Don't be afraid. Ask for the channel to be pure. We are all prophets, all Gnostics, all speakers of truth. God has chosen us, and we are very blessed. We are chosen, and we must stay chosen. We cannot get off the spiritual path.

We are beating a new path, a path through weeds and ignorance and fear, but we are strong. For as long as I am around, I will carry that banner. When I am not, you must carry the banner, because it is deep-seated in your soul.

We want to make the world a better place. We want to make souls well. We want to turn the darkness into light, wherever we go. Feel that light come on; feel it burn through; feel that your soul begins to magnify; feel that your heart is healed; feel that your soul grows strong.

We ask this in the name of Father, Mother, Jesus, and the Holy Spirit.

Bring yourself up to yourself.

The Mission of Gnosticism

It has occurred to me over the years of doing readings, starting the church, wanting to walk in the light of God, and fulfilling my mission, that the mission is so simple that we often bypass it.

Our mission is just to live and exist and to do good.

We make it so complicated. We also get focus on certain things. I see it happen all the time. I, myself, have to watch out because I can be guilty of that. We get one thing in our mind: "I want that man.

I want that job. I will never be happy until I get it." With me, it was, "I won't be happy until we have a church." When we get these blinders on, it wrecks our spirituality. What we have to do is give that to God and let it go.

People often ask what our beliefs are as Gnostics. We believe that you come back many times, until you learn that life must be filled with the mission of experiencing for God. And in turn, you get it back. And we believe in not making so much of this world, compared to the Other Side.

The Gnostics say, "In your own heart resides the truth." When you come together and meet, you bring your own truth. Then a collective truth grows about loving God and showing Him what we are doing. We write down petitions to Azna—not because Azna demands or is limited by certain things, but only because in that way, you program your soul. You're doing something active.

You lift your soul. The more you program, act smart, be smart, and act confident, you become those very things.

Gnostics believe in not only searching for the knowledge, but spreading it and getting rid of devils and darkness and hate and prejudice. I was talking to one of my ministers today. She was relating to me that in groups, there are egos. There will always be issues of ego. Francine, my guide, says, "Get three people together in a room, and you've got a universe of every type of problem—not only from this life, but from many lives."

Every messenger who has come has said, "Love your neighbor, love yourself, do good works, and go Home." Then the multitudes who followed wrote volumes of literature on what that messenger *really* meant.

How many times in this life have we all prayed, and then we said, "God didn't answer my prayer." We've said that, haven't we? That's not God's job. Did anybody ever tell you that? That is not God's job. *You* wrote the contract. But then, when you got down here, you got frustrated and said, "Wait a minute. I don't want to do this anymore," the same as Jesus did on Gethsemane. Sorry. We all made our own contract, and then we got mad, saying, "God didn't listen." Well, God *did* actually answer your prayer. It just happens that the answer turned out to be "No."

Or people say, "I don't have any companions." Wouldn't it be nice to have a companion along the way? Yes, but then who are all of us sitting here—chopped liver? Who are you sitting next to? Who loves you unconditionally, like God does? We do.

My grandmother used to say, "If you live long enough, you'll see everything." Isn't that a pleasant thought? But pray to God that we have the strength and the courage to endure it.

How many times have we said, "Be careful what you pray for, you may get it"? We pray for someone who is ill, "Please make them all right," and they die. Don't you see? They *are* all right. Why do you think God doesn't answer your prayers? Because if you'd gotten your wish, it would have been a nightmare.

LIGHT MEDITATION

Let's put the purple light around us today, which is highly spiritual and cements our intellect and emotion. Feel now the peace of the brilliant purple light around us as it breathes and pulsates. The world is made of color and light, and it was put there for a purpose.

Let's feel that on a sandy beach, as it says in the poem, "Jesus not only walks with us, but will also carry us." So can we, in turn, carry Jesus in our heart. Feel right through the middle of your forehead, a beautiful burning Light coming directly from God the Father, rinsing out all the fears, desires, and resentments. Let them go. It's just so much junk from this life anyway. In its place, expand your heart and your consciousness to the love of God that fills every single cell.

Across the sand now, appears a bridge that we can cross only in our thoughts, but someday in reality. The bridge to the Other Side—to Home, where everyone is waving to us in greeting. All our animals that have passed, all the loved ones, your dear sweet guide standing there, all the ancestors, everyone from the Other Side.

The party begins—life begins, and death ends. This life fades into oblivion, like the bad dream that it was. Except that what is left is the strength that you've garnered from it, and as I always say, your "white plume" was unsullied by greed and the wrongs done against you. Let those go.

Be filled with the love of God; nothing can take its place. Feel your soul magnify now and stretch. When you truly give it up to God, it all comes rushing in—peace of mind. The addictions and the needs fall away. All the prejudices of color and creed fall away. Love, by its golden hand, sweeps away all the cobwebs of guilt and darkness and suspicion and disbelief.

Take a deep breath, and release all the negativity. Keep around you Mother and Father God, the love of the Holy Spirit that swirls as your companion, and the Golden Sword of Azna with which you can cut away all negativity.

On the count of three, bring yourself all the way up. One, two, three.

Please hold fast and steady with me. Please know that I'm always here with you. I would hate to think that all this was done, and that we lived and died for nothing, wouldn't you? Within our heart, we must show the light to people. Not because of their salvation—because they're already going to be saved— but to ease their minds while they're here. God love you and protect you and keep you.

Missing the Mark

The Greek word rendered as *sin* is far less frightening than the modern English version. Also, it may not have been quite so cursed and polluted a word as *sin* is. Literally, in Aramaic, *sin* means "missing the mark."

It means aiming at something perceived as good, but judging wrong (picking the wrong targets) and not shooting straight. For the reason just given, and not to minimize the importance of human action for good or evil, the translation usually speaks of errors *against oneself.* As for the "sinners," the term would apply not just to the authors of real crimes, but to anyone who was not a good, practicing Jew.

You must think, because you are Gnostics. People are so willing to accept whatever comes out of someone's mouth, rather than research the original texts. Maybe we will not really know what the original texts said, but we have to think and research enough to know that God did put us down here to love others and survive "hell."

Don't you see? Even the Creation myth of Adam and Eve keeps repeating itself in every culture. There is always a "first man and woman." If Adam and Eve were to gain knowledge, they had to be put on Earth, because you cannot have knowledge without experience.

The only way that anyone can experience for God, as we are pledged to, is to go down and toil in the fields. I could talk at length to you about what childbirth is like, but if you haven't experienced it, you might very well say, "Sounds interesting, but I still can't imagine it."

We're all fingers of God that move. The deeper you love, the deeper into spirituality you become, and the harder you're hit by each experience. The deeper your love goes for the ultimate beloved Mother and Father God, the more exquisite the pain becomes in its agony. The deeper it goes, the more we want to go Home and be joined with God again, to be wrapped in His arms.

PRAYER MEDITATION

Dear God,

We ask for your immediacy in giving us blessings today. We ask for Mother God to wrap us in Her mantle of protection. We ask for the God Consciousness to walk beside us and in our heart.

We make a pledge today. We will follow the path of Jesus. We will follow the path of all the Anointed Ones, who try to bring peace and harmony and love. Let no person spoil the fact that we are now pure of heart and spirit.

We remove all hurt and fear, and stand before God as a

shining, pure, crystal light. We ask only for strength. We ask only for fortitude. We ask that there be a funnel by which our spirituality comes through—not through our suffering, but through our strength. We rid ourselves of empathy.

We ask to put on the fighting mantle of truth, because as it has been said so many times, "Truth will set you free."

Now, feel the warm baptism of healing coming directly from the Mother God, who is the Great Interceptor; from Jesus, who was an Anointed One on this earth; from the Father God, who holds us continuously in His hands. Ask that the journey be made easier, but more important, that we have the strength of conviction. We are witnesses to the truth.

Say in your heart, "Blessed be Thy name."

Don't be afraid to say to God today, "I love You. You are my creator, consummator, healer, lover, and benefactor. For You, oh God, all of this is for You. Through my soul, I will magnify that. In doing that, I will be healed. When it comes time for me to go, I will cross over that threshold blissfully, happily, and be in the presence of Your marvelous and magnificent force. I will carry the embodiment of Jesus with me throughout this life. I ask this in the name of the Mother and the Father, and the Holy Spirit's light that guides me through this dark world."

Bring yourself up—all the way up with strength and purpose and fight.

✑ About the Author ✑

*Millions of people have witnessed **Sylvia Browne's** incredible psychic powers on TV shows such as **Montel, Larry King Live, Entertainment Tonight,** and **Unsolved Mysteries;** and she has been profiled in **Cosmopolitan, People** magazine, and other national media. Her on-target psychic readings have helped police solve crimes, and she astounds audiences wherever she appears.*

ė ė ė

Contact Sylvia Browne at:
www.sylvia.org
or
Sylvia Browne Corporation
35 Dillon Ave.
Campbell, CA 95008
(408) 379-7070

Other Hay House Titles of Related Interest

BOOKS

Born to Be Together: *Love Relationships, Astrology, and the Soul,*
by Terry Lamb

Colors & Numbers:
Your Personal Guide to Positive Vibrations in Daily Life,
by Louise L. Hay

The Experience of God:
How 40 Well-Known Seekers Encounter the Sacred,
edited by Jonathan Robinson

Experiencing the Soul:
Before Birth, During Life, After Death,
by Eliot Jay Rosen

Infinite Self:
33 Steps to Reclaiming Your Inner Power,
by Stuart Wilde

The Lightworker's Way:
Awakening Your Spiritual Power to Know and Heal,
by Doreen Virtue, Ph.D.

Magi Astrology™:
The Key to Success in Love and Money,
by The Magi Society®

AUDIO PROGRAMS

Developing Your Own Psychic Powers,
by John Edward

Psychic and Intuitive Healing,
by Barbara Brennan, Rosalyn Bruyere, and Judith Orloff, M.D.,
with Michael Toms

Unleashing Your Psychic Potential,
by John Edward

Understanding Your Angels and Meeting Your Guides,
by John Edward

§ § § ‒ ‒ ‒

We hope you enjoyed this Hay House book.
If you would like to receive a free catalog featuring additional
Hay House books and products, or if you would like information
about the Hay Foundation, please contact:

Hay House, Inc.
P.O. Box 5100
Carlsbad, CA 92018-5100

(760) 431-7695 or **(800) 654-5126**
(760) 431-6948 (fax) or **(800) 650-5115 (fax)**

Please visit the Hay House Website at: **hayhouse.com**

§ § § ‒ ‒ ‒

THIS IS THE NEWSLETTER YOU'VE BEEN WAITING FOR . . .

Find out
SYLVIA BROWNE'S
secrets for developing
your psychic powers!

Order your charter subscription today to the *Sylvia Browne Newsletter*, and receive an exclusive lecture tape from Psychic Sylvia Browne—absolutely **FREE!**

Now is your chance to hear from your favorite author and psychic Sylvia Browne—six times a year—in the pages of this remarkable new newsletter!

As a charter subscriber to the newsletter, you'll learn inside information directly from Sylvia Browne. You'll find out how to **connect with your angels,** learn about the **Other Side,** and get Sylvia's latest **predictions** as well as information on how to **get and stay healthy.**

You'll be the first to hear about **the latest psychic discoveries** of Sylvia or her psychic son, **Chris Dufresne.** Also, your charter subscription allows you to **write to Sylvia** whenever you want, and as often as you like —and one of your questions may be featured in an upcoming newsletter along with Sylvia's answer.

Send for your Charter Subscription and FREE lecture tape today!

IN A RUSH? Call **800-654-5126,** or fax postcard to **800-650-5115!**
www.hayhouse.com

Fold along dotted line.

Exclusive Sylvia Browne Lecture Tape—FREE!
With one-year subscription to *The Sylvia Browne Newsletter*

❏ **YES!** Enter my one-year subscription to *Sylvia Browne's Newsletter* today at the low introductory rate of $19.95, and send my FREE lecture tape immediately. I understand that I may cancel this subscription at any time for a full refund for remaining newsletters, and that the free gift is mine to keep.

Name_____

Address_____

City, State, Zip_____

Phone _____

E-mail _____   _____
(I authorize Hay House to send me information via e-mail)

Method of Payment:
❏ Visa ❏ MasterCard ❏ AmEx ❏ Discover ❏ Check or Money Order
Card No._____ Exp. Date_____

Signature_____

Please tape closed. Do not staple.

Exclusive
SYLVIA BROWNE
Lecture Tape—FREE!

With one-year subscription

Fold along dotted line.